GREENING YOUR HOME

Successful Eco-Renovation Strategies

**Thomas Teuwen &
Laura L. Parker**

Self-Counsel Press
(a division of)
International Self-Counsel Press Ltd.
USA   Canada

Self-Counsel Press acknowledges the financial support of the Government of Canada through the Canada Book Fund for our publishing activities.

Printed in Canada.

First edition: 2014

Library and Archives Canada Cataloguing in Publication

Teuwen, Thomas, author

Greening your home : successful eco-renovation strategies / Thomas Teuwen and Laura Parker.

(Self-Counsel green series)

Issued in print and electronic formats.

ISBN 978-1-77040-207-2 (pbk.).—ISBN 978-1-77040-962-0 (epub).— ISBN 978-1-77040-963-7 (kindle)

1. Energy conservation. 2. Ecological houses. 3. Sustainable living. I. Parker, Laura (Laura Lynn), author II. Title. III. Series: Self-Counsel green series

TJ163.3.T48 2014   643'.1   C2014-905611-7

Self-Counsel Press
(a division of)
International Self-Counsel Press Ltd.
Bellingham, WA   North Vancouver, BC
USA   Canada

Contents

Notice to Readers

Laws are constantly changing. Every effort is made to keep this publication as current as possible. However, the author, the publisher, and the vendor of this book make no representations or warranties regarding the outcome or the use to which the information in this book is put and are not assuming any liability for any claims, losses, or damages arising out of the use of this book. The reader should not rely on the author or the publisher of this book for any professional advice. Please be sure that you have the most recent edition.

Acknowledgments

We would like to thank Anne-Marie Daniel for introducing us to Kirk LaPointe and Self-Counsel Press. To our editors Tanya Lee Howe and Eileen Velthuis, thank you for challenging us to be the best writers that we can be. Thank you also to Tracey Bhangu in Publicity and Tyler Douglas in Marketing for getting the word out about this book; that we can all make a difference in our everyday lives.

To our building, plumbing, and electrical inspectors, thank you for being our parachute as we embarked on our own building adventures. Thank you to all those who have come before us and who have encouraged us to do the right thing by building green.

Mostly, we want to thank you, the reader, for picking up this book because you care. It is you who holds the future of our marvelous civilization in your hands. Like the raindrop that feeds the river on its way to the ocean, it is your individual decisions that will drive change. Thank you for your commitment to doing the right thing and for your willingness to learn new concepts and explore new ideas. Thank you for having the courage to try.

— Thomas and Laura

Introduction

Building green is not a new idea. While the concept of our carbon footprint and the focus on carbon reduction is fairly recent, many architects and builders have been aware of the environmental consequences of their decisions since the 1970s. Back then, the focus tended to be on pollution and the toxicity of materials, both inside the home and in their places of processing or manufacturing.

During the oil shock of the 1970s, the push to insulate homes was mostly driven by economic considerations and all types of materials were injected into exterior wall cavities, including the dreaded asbestos. Not only was asbestos included in blown-in insulation but it was also embedded in tiles, sheet flooring, and drywall. There were many false starts, and more than a few dead ends on the road to sustainability, some of which turned out to be disastrous and expensive to remediate.

Insulation without proper vapor barriers proved to be functionally short lived as it absorbs moisture condensing inside the walls. Vapor barriers without proper ventilation proved treacherous as it increases the humidity in the home to the point of triggering uncontrolled and often very unhealthy mold growth. Ventilation without heat recovery soon negates much of the benefit of the insulation.

A home built at the turn of the last century was inherently drafty. The inside of the studs and joists tended to be covered with lath and plaster, put there by an arduous process of nailing thin furring strips perpendicular to the studs with gaps of the right proportions to allow the plaster to be squeezed through, expand, or deform slightly, and hook itself into place.

The outside cladding would typically consist of one layer of planking followed by a layer of birch bark, cardboard, or tar paper, on top of which was placed another layer of shiplap siding. Windows were single pane although the frugal among us might have mounted shutters to be closed during storms or at night.

Storm windows that, in the beginning, would be removed in spring and stored until fall were perhaps the first attempt at improving the energy efficiency of a home. It may have become popular because one of the side benefits of installing these often unsightly aluminum additions was that they prevented condensation and ice buildup on the inside of a single-pane window, which allowed for a clear view during the winter months.

Homes in the last century typically housed large and often extended families. Three, four, and even five bedrooms were commonplace. Kitchens were utilitarian, a place where "women folk" or sometimes servants did the messy work. They were usually situated at the back of the house, hidden from view and fully segregated from the stately dining rooms where as many as 10 or 12 people would gather around at mealtime.

Amazingly, these densely populated, 2,500-square-foot homes often were outfitted with only one water closet, usually separate from the bathroom to maximize its accessibility. Vertical slider windows would provide any desired ventilation and a minimum of one "naturally aspiring, fuel fired vented appliance" (as the building code refers to it now) consisting of a wood or coal stove was present to help suck the stale air out of the building.

We remind ourselves of this history to illustrate that much of our current design and building practices have their roots firmly planted in the legacy of the past. There is a story that is told of a little girl who is watching intently as her mother prepares dinner one afternoon. After the onions and carrots are cut into cubes, the mother carefully unwraps the roast, places it on a cutting board and before nestling it into the pan trims off the ends with a sharp knife.

The little girl, resting her chin on her fist as she peeks over the edge of the counter, asks innocently: "Mommy, why do you cut the ends off the roast before placing it into the pan?"

"You know darling, I'm not sure. I've always done it this way because that's how I learned it when I was a little girl. Let's go visit your Nana tomorrow and ask her."

"Nana, Nana, we've come to ask you a question!," the little girl was so excited to be on this quest that she announced their reason for the visit before welcoming hugs were exchanged. "I asked Mommy why she cuts the ends off the roast before putting it in the pan, and she said she learned it from you! Why did you do that, Nana?"

"Good question my child," was the immediate response. "I suppose I learned it from your Great Grandma. Let's call her and ask her shall we?"

The phone rang a good long time before the old woman answered it. But the little girl was patient. "Grandma?"

"Yes darling, how wonderful of you to call!"

"Grandma, I watched Mommy cut the ends off her roast yesterday and she told me that is how she learned it from Nana. Then Nana told me that is how she learned it from you. Why, Grandma, why did you cut the ends off the roast before you put it in the pan?"

"Why that's easy, my darling, I only had one pan and the roast was always too big, so I cut off the ends to make it fit!"

Just because something has been done a certain way for generations does not mean it's the most appropriate method for the times. Humans are not hardwired to cope easily with change. We prefer the well-worn patterns of habit to the treacherous realm of innovation. Tradespeople, designers, and architects tend to build on past practices; often old concepts are simply adapted to new situations without considering their genesis or even their underlying purpose. Of course, it's important to build on the knowledge of the past but this should never dissuade us from asking why, and exploring the deeper issues underlying accepted practices.

We have come a long way since double-pane windows were invented in the 1930s. Over the years improved methods of draft proofing and insulating our homes have reduced our energy requirements. We have learned about energy-efficient appliances and even as we convert our lightbulbs to compact fluorescent lamps (CFL) we recognize that new light-emitting diode (LED) lighting is taking the industry by storm.

We know that turning down our thermostat a couple of degrees and installing low-flow showerheads can save us money on our energy bills. Many of us have at least considered the energy savings of heat pumps and passive solar strategies. For decades now, countless books and magazine articles have touted these "baby steps" to greening our homes.

In this book we want to reach a little further. We start with the premise that your situation is unique, but that you are already aware of the need to reduce your carbon footprint. From there we explore some of the less obvious issues of green design and construction. It is not our intention to focus on specific solutions. Circumstances change from region to region and the best practices of today may be superseded by the new technologies of tomorrow.

Save for a few sojourns into the anecdotes of our building adventures, we will focus on the broader perspective of sustainability. We will explore the hidden carbon and economic costs of bad design and poor practices, and offer you more than a checklist of the right things to do. Our objective is to focus on strategies that you can readily adapt to your circumstances. We want you to develop familiarity with the issues so that whether you do the work yourself or hire experienced professionals, the end result will meet your objectives and expectations.

No doubt you are keen to proceed with turning your ideals into reality. So let's explore the concept of embodied energy and get you started on the right foot as you embark on your eco-renovation!

Note: The forms and checklists included in this book are also provided on the download kit so that you can easily print and use them. See the last page of this book for access to the kit.

1
The Carbon Footprint of Embodied Energy

"You cannot get through a single day without having an impact on the world around you. What you do makes a difference, and you have to decide what kind of difference you want to make."

— Jane Goodall, Ethologist and Zoologist

When we speak of greening our home the first question we are always asked is, "Do you have solar panels on your roof?" Of course solar is a hot topic and as we will discuss in Chapter 8, it has many benefits to help make your home green. However, there is more to the story. Even the second most frequent question, "Is your house super insulated?" leaves out a major element of building and renovating green: Embodied energy.

Before we explore this often overlooked impact on the environment, let's review the operational carbon footprint of a Canadian home. The most obvious is the energy we consume to heat and cool our houses.

According to the Statistics Canada 2011 report entitled, "Households and the Environment: Energy Use,"[1] the total consumption of household energy was about 1.4 million terajoules. This was comprised of electricity (38 percent), natural gas (45 percent), and heating oil (4 percent). Wood, propane, and other energy sources made up the remaining 13 percent. Only 1 percent of households used alternative energy sources such as solar and wind.

In 2011 the average Canadian household consumed 105 gigajoules (GJ) of energy per year. Converted to something we can all understand, this represents about 29,000 kilowatt hours (kWh) per household. That's enough electricity to run 29,000, 1,000-watt baseboard heaters for one hour. Clearly a lot of energy.

Predictably, more occupants per household reduced the energy consumption per capita and households in the top income category consumed twice the energy of households in the bottom. Surprisingly, university educated Canadians used 25 percent more energy per household than those who failed to graduate from high school and the average energy consumption per household varied little with the age of the home. Houses built between 1946 and 1960 averaged 104 gigajoules per household, whereas houses built after 1996 averaged 111.

Since the energy consumption per square meter of a heated area dropped by 16 percent for the same period, no doubt due to the increased efficiency of appliances and improved insulating practices, the reason for the overall increase in energy consumption was a clear trend toward larger homes. The good news is that this trend has started to reverse itself. More and more designers are realizing that not all our living space has to be inside the home and that more efficient use of space can yield huge dividends.

Still, there is much room for improvement in our heating, ventilation, and insulation practices. In 2011, even our lighting was mostly outdated; 41 percent of lightbulbs used in Canada were incandescent and 22 percent were halogen, both high-energy consumers especially when compared to the LED lights now so readily available.

Natural Resources Canada reports that about 60 percent of the energy required by the average home is used for space heating. (In the southern US this might be air conditioning instead.) The second most demanding appliance is your hot water heater, consuming about 20 percent of our annual energy demand. Naturally any green makeover should include insulating and draft proofing against the heat and the

---

1 "Households and the Environment: Energy Use," Statistics Canada 2011 report, accessed September 2014. http://www.statcan.gc.ca/pub/11-526-s/11-526-s2013002-eng.htm

cold but you may also want to make a super insulated hot water tank and/or a thermal solar water heating system a priority.

There are many burgeoning technologies to consider but the most effective way to make your home as green as possible is to limit its size. Not only does a smaller home reduce the amount of energy it takes to operate but it also reduces the other main contribution to its carbon footprint: Embodied energy.

Note: As does the US Energy Information Administration, Statistics Canada periodically compiles very useful information on household energy use. We use Canadian statistics here as an example because most of the country lives along the 49th parallel and experiences similar climates to the US. You may want to use regional statistics where you live. California is very different from New York State and, when looking for improvements, it helps to know what your neighbors have already been able to achieve.

Be careful when you evaluate statistics. Read the fine print and make sure you understand what the sampling really represents. For example, it's not very useful to combine heating statistics for Alaska and Arizona when you are trying to set the bar for your heating load.

1. What Is Embodied Energy?

Embodied energy is the sum of all the energy required to produce the components that make up your house. Wikipedia describes it as "an accounting method which aims to find the sum total of the energy necessary for an entire product life cycle including raw material extraction, transport, manufacture, assembly, installation, disassembly, deconstruction and/or decomposition, as well as human and secondary resources."[2] Estimates vary but the amount of embodied energy as a percentage of the total energy consumption of your home can range from as low as 25 percent to more than 50 percent.

Because we still produce most of our energy by burning fossil fuels, energy consumption equals carbon emissions. The total carbon footprint of your home is greatly influenced by the amount of energy it took to build it. Here is the catch; if you don't build to last, the embodied energy in your project can counteract any benefits from that added insulation or that gleaming new solar panel.

2. Hidden Energy Consumption

Let's take a closer look at hidden energy consumption. Everything in your home, every nail, hinge, piece of glass, board, and piece of copper

---

2 "Embodied energy" definition according to Wikipedia, accessed September 2014.
   http://en.wikipedia.org/wiki/Embodied_energy

wire behind the drywall consumed energy to manufacture, distribute, and transport to the job site. It can be an eye-opening exercise to follow the supply chain back to its beginning. Take nails for instance. If you wander through a modern construction site you will often see clips of them lying about in the mud and hundreds scattered across the plywood subfloor.

The humble nail that you buy at the hardware store has its beginnings in an iron ore mine such as the one in Labrador City, Newfoundland. To extract the iron from the ore and turn it into steel requires a blast furnace capable of reaching temperatures of up to 5,400 degrees Fahrenheit (3,000 Celsius). This is accomplished by burning a coal derivative called "coke" and in the process emitting large sums of CO^2. Almost 70 percent of the world's steel consumption is still produced this way.

The remaining 30 percent is produced in electric arc furnaces using primarily scrap steel which has been recovered from previous uses but which originated in a blast furnace. Red hot bars are extruded from the liquid steel, and then a series of rolling mills reduce the bars to the diameter of wire. Another machine, usually located far from the mill, uses this wire as a feedstock to cut and shape the common nail.

All these processes, the industrial plants and factories that house them, the employees who operate them, as well as the cranes and trucks that transport the final product to us, depend on the consumption of carbon emitting energy. The carbon footprint of a nail is the cumulative carbon emissions of this supply chain amortized over the useful lifespan of the nail.

Another example is the asphalt shingle roof. Sometimes also called composite roofing since the underlying wood fiber-felt substrate has increasingly been replaced with a fibrous glass mat. Both rely on tar and by the time asphalt shingles were invented in 1901 the natural tar used for eons as a sealing and preserving agent had been largely replaced by coal tar, a by-product of the process.

Tar shingles naturally contain polycyclic aromatic hydrocarbons (PAHs) which are known carcinogens that can leach out and contaminate rainwater. For this reason alone, they do not belong on a sustainably built home that aims to capture and store water for use in the garden. While more than 12 million tons of asphalt shingle waste is generated in the United States and Canada each year, the shingles are difficult to recycle and almost all end up in landfills.

Now that we are firmly planted in the twenty-first century it's high time we leave this wasteful technology behind and focus on the new materials now available. From recycled plastic to solar tiles, from clay shingles to metal roofing, there are many alternatives that will outperform asphalt in the long run and reduce the embedded carbon component of your roof substantially. Metal roofing has the added bonus of being fully recyclable into more metal roofing since it is easy to disassemble and return to the steel mill as feedstock.

When we consider all the materials that go into building a house or addition and follow their individual supply chains, it soon becomes clear that there are many opportunities to green your project by making informed design and purchasing decisions. The embodied energy component extends beyond the cumulative energy requirement of delivering the materials to your site and reaches decades into the future to their final disposal.

What determines the life span of a house? Some say a house can last forever as long as the owner does the necessary maintenance. Others point out that a house becomes obsolete as soon as its owners decide that what it offers no longer satisfies their needs. Along this spectrum, somewhere between these two extremes, lies the complex reality of how long a house will last before it faces demolition.

Your house may well be the biggest investment you will ever make. Naturally, it is prudent to protect its value by making sure it stays in good shape. This goes beyond replacing the leaky hot water tank and curled up shingles from time to time. It reaches deeper than a coat of paint or changing drafty windows.

There is a natural process all around us that clearly delineates between growth and decay. Organic matter is either alive and growing or it is dead and decaying. Inorganic matter is either being formed or breaking down. Since we don't build our dwellings out of growing and forming materials, they are naturally in a state of deterioration. We can slow down that process but we can't stop it.

When thinking sustainably, there is another dimension to this picture. Nature teaches us that the deterioration of all things is a good thing. A dying tree in the forest need not be removed and replaced. It houses a whole ecosystem of life that uses it as food and shelter for years before it falls to the ground. As it continues to rot it helps make fresh soil for new trees to grow. Literally every aspect of the natural world is in a constant state of deterioration, filled with opportunity for newness to reemerge.

When we build or renovate sustainably we do well to be aware of this process. We do this by considering the complete life cycle of not only our house but of every component that makes up its structure and form. This can be a daunting task and seem overwhelming at first but it need not be. A simple awareness of this principle applied when the opportunity presents itself, will steer your many decisions towards a more sustainable outcome.

The biosphere is a closed system from which nothing escapes. There is no "away" to throw things. Everything you purchase for or consume in your home will form part of the environment for future generations somewhere on our planet. This can be in the form of trash or it can be in the form of a legacy that you can be proud of.

Perhaps one of the first questions to ask yourself is how long should your renovation last? Having taken the initiative to explore sustainable renovation practices you have undoubtedly already progressed past the notion of instant gratification. You may be well acquainted with the sentiment of the "Great Law of the Iroquois," that we should consider the impact of what we do at least seven generations into the future. Maximum sustainability will be achieved if your renovation not only lasts as long as the rest of the house but contributes to extending the life span of the home by making it more resilient and more livable.

In North America the average life span of a residential dwelling is estimated at between 40 and 65 years. In Europe it's easily twice that. Some of that is cultural for sure, but a lot has to do with the choice of materials. For example, new subdivisions and old walled cities share the predominant feature of extremely durable clay tile roofs. Still, one would be hard pressed to find a home more than 40 years old, on either side of the Atlantic, which has not been through at least one major renovation.

Determining the "effective age" of your house is a great starting point when planning your eco-renovation. Perhaps it's still in its youth, simply having gotten off to a bad start. Maybe it's tired and neglected, too crippled to be rejuvenated. Or maybe it's simply facing a profound midlife crisis and, with a little brilliance on your part, can look forward to growing old gracefully.

3. Explore Functionality of Current Design

Renovating sustainably involves exploring the functionality of your current design. Of course, sometimes it requires an addition be built. Often it is more effective to reconfigure the layout of your home, changing the emphasis of living spaces and adapting them to our modern lifestyles. Some architects are now designing smaller homes with this idea in mind. By using advanced materials and techniques to maximize the span of floors and ceilings, they eliminate the need for interior supporting walls. This makes it possible to renovate extensively and redesign the layout as the home owner's needs and circumstances change.

Sustainable renovation provides an opportunity to reach beyond the simplistic approach of adding more space to store more stuff and explore ways of reducing your carbon footprint while making your home more livable. It may even call for a reduction in the total square footage of your house which can result in a saving of operational costs and, in some instances, maintenance costs as well.

It may also include facilitating sustainable lifestyle strategies such as growing more of your own food or housing bicycles in a conveniently dry and secure part of your home. Both of these adaptations, while not reducing the carbon footprint directly, can help to offset it by encouraging you to reduce the carbon costs of your food and transportation.

4. Where to Draw the Line

When renovating, it is very important to know where to draw the line; generating a smooth transition between old and new offers fantastic opportunities for artistic expression. It's such an important design consideration that it should be addressed early in the project. The transition from old to new must not always be hidden. Highlighting the contrast underscores your commitment to sustainability by demonstrating how to make things last. Remember that everything eventually ends up at the dump and delaying this can extend the amortization of your home's embodied carbon footprint.

One technique that can be used to facilitate this transition is to apply a textured drywall finish. For some inexplicable reason we have become obsessed with clinically smooth, perfectly flat interior wall cladding. It may have started when we invented gypsum board and replaced the textured plaster in our homes with factory produced panels. It may have seemed like the "modern look" in the same way that there was a time when frozen TV dinners were considered modern food.

Do we have to perpetuate this obsession? Clearly not. Making drywall smooth and flat is extremely wasteful. It requires that we minimize the number of seams which increases drywall scrap to ludicrous levels. The National Association of Home Builders in the US calculates that the construction of a 2,000-square-foot home produces 8,000 pounds of waste, most of it wood and drywall (www.epa. gov/wastes/inforesources/pubs/infocus/nf-cd.pdf, accessed October, 2014). When we built our 1,250-square-foot home (750-square-foot footprint) we reused practically all of our scrap lumber multiple times and produced less than two garbage pails of drywall. Here is how we did it.

First, we realized that splicing drywall on studs is tricky business. Studs are never exactly on center and they are seldom exactly straight. So while the pretty pictures in some how-to books show a drywall splice running down the center of a stud, leaving you three-quarters of an inch to attach the edge of the panel, in real life it's seldom that easy. Walls are often framed with studs that have a slight twist or bow and 16-inch centers are not always diligently observed. Sometimes the studs are milled close to the edge of the tree and still have some bark on them which takes away from the contact surface.

We decided to simply let the drywall progress in full sheets and fasten a scrap of three-quarter-inch board as backing to the splice — less cutting, less measuring, and less scrap. Then we used fiberglass tape for the seams because for the DIY handyperson it's much easier to work with and will never blister or lift. Finally, instead of the endless and dreaded sanding of drywall compound we simply applied the compound in broad, free-flowing strokes to create a textured finish that's a snap to repair.

In nature, there are no truly flat planes. Everything has texture and form. Textures scatter the light and create unexpected shades and hues as the day progresses into night. Just like the old poplar tree in our backyard whose leaves sparkle in the wind as they flash their silvery underside, so our pure white walls constantly change in appearance as they reflect the light of the glulam beams, the colorful furniture, or even the dress of the occupants, in their shifting shadows.

Creating a striking transition from old to new can be a blast and it can go way beyond the style of the wall covering you choose. Be creative, be bold, and be remarkable.

Who said that all the trim in the house has to match or the flooring has to be contiguous? Often a simple line can separate one living space from another while making both spaces appear larger. The line does not have to be straight or predictable. Sometimes that line is not even visible. By its very nature, a renovation requires a transition from old to new. Getting a firm grip on where that line is drawn can save you a lot of time, money, and frustration in the end.

How often have we heard the justification, "But it has good bones!" after a renovation has gotten out of hand? The wood framing of a typical North American home usually makes up only about 10 percent of the cost of construction. Since every component of a home requires carbon emitting energy to produce, and energy is expensive, stripping down a house to its framing while maintaining an outdated and dysfunctional layout makes little sense.

Still, there are good reasons we should consider the condition of the framing first, especially if you are sure that you want to maintain the current floor plan. Failing studs or plates may require replacing before you can do anything else. Alternatively, if the "bones" are good, you may be able to proceed in stages or phases, selectively addressing yourself to inside and outside cladding as budgets permit.

Another reason to inspect the structural members early is that this may offer clues to the success of the existing cladding and other materials in withstanding the challenges of local conditions. For example, there is a pest that infests older homes in some parts of North America whose acquaintance we made while deconstructing our old house. The wood-boring beetle spends most of its life cycle as larvae inside the framing lumber. Similar to termites, the beetle prefers moist conditions, but once it gets established will spread to dryer sections. The only clues to its presence are a few tiny holes in the timbers where the adult briefly escapes to lay eggs. The larvae, upon hatching, immediately disappear back into the wood. It is quite common to have a dimensionally perfect two-by-four so hollowed out that a child can break it in two.

If you find a serious infestation of these beetles, you likely have a moisture problem that needs to be assessed before you go any further. Not all moisture problems stem from leaks. We will address some of the more serious ones caused by condensation and errant dew points in Chapter 4. As a rule, the best place to look for moisture and check the integrity of your framing is in the attic and wherever you can gain access to the bottom of a first-story exterior wall cavity.

Sometimes this involves removing some drywall. Determining the structural integrity of your home is important. Whether you investigate it yourself or hire a professional to do an assessment, it is well worth the effort and cost. It will provide you with a sense of comfort and some assurance that your finished project can be enjoyed for many years to come, allowing the carbon footprint to be amortized over decades.

What if your renovation turns out to be a compromise that still leaves the house wanting? What if only a few years later you decide that it's too dark, too cramped, or too cumbersome in its layout? What if your choice of materials, fixtures, and trim don't match the perceived value of the home? What if the execution of the renovation lacks the attention to detail that gives it that sense of permanence?

If perfectly good cabinets are removed after only two or three years of service to make room for that grand archway that invites guests into your kitchen, or if that new tub simply does not fit into a larger, more accessible master bathroom that befits the income bracket of a prospective buyer, the renovation could be a colossal failure from an environmental point of view.

Shoddy, poorly designed, and compromising renovations are probably the biggest contributors to the embodied carbon footprint of a house. If the life of a kitchen is cut in half because of poor layout or some other major shortcoming, its embodied carbon footprint is doubled. Should you find yourself at the receiving end of this scenario it is helpful if you cart your used fixtures and cabinets to a recycling facility (e.g., Habitat for Humanity ReStore) or give them to an enterprising couple who is willing to give these components a second life.

When we built our new home we were at the receiving end of such a transaction. A friend of a friend was undergoing a kitchen renovation and removed a perfectly functional double sink which we inherited. Laura used a wire wheel at the end of a drill gun to take the scratches out and her loving care gave it that hand-brushed finish that is usually offered as an expensive upgrade in showrooms.

We also salvaged the Douglas fir flooring in the old house and repurposed it as stair treads in our new home. By preserving the natural patina of the old wood with some sanding sealer and adding a newly milled bull-nose we were able to contrast the old with the new in a stunning display of the longevity of this fine wood. Douglas fir actually gets harder with age; while being fairly easy to mill when new, it can rival some hardwoods for durability.

Salvaging old and used materials is a great way to reduce the embodied carbon footprint of your renovation, but in the end it's not enough. For a greening approach to be fully sustainable it needs to be replicable. We have more than 7 billion people on this planet and if we are serious about reducing our carbon emissions globally, we must all play our part in identifying working solutions that everyone can employ with satisfying results.

When it comes to reducing the embodied carbon footprint of your home, it's important to remember that everything requires energy to produce. Until we progress to harvesting all our energy from the sun in a sustainable way, energy consumption still produces the carbon emissions that drive climate change and ocean acidification.

Let's explore how we can maximize our living space, and build great homes with smaller footprints for a better tomorrow!

2
Maximizing the Livable Space in Your Home

"There is nothing more uncommon than common sense."

— Frank Lloyd Wright, Architect

For most people, renovation means the expansion of their living space to satisfy a personal need or changing circumstances. All too often though, the cramped feeling that our clutter induces is addressed by simply adding more space to store it — a studio, a playroom, a den, or maybe a "great room." Instead of adding a great room, why not consider transforming your home into a "great house"? As Jill Eisen pointed out 15 years ago, we are all drowning in stuff and it all ends up at the dump.[1] If your eco-renovation can induce you to eliminate the unused stuff in your life, it will be a measurable success by reducing your carbon footprint on that front alone.

Since you are on the path to living more sustainably you have probably already explored ideas on how to de-clutter your life, so we won't spend a lot of time on that here. However, it is an important factor to consider when planning your eco-renovation. Are you remodeling

---

1 *Drowning in Stuff*, Audiobook, by Jill Eisen. Publisher: Canadian Broadcasting Corporation (CBC Audio), March 2000.

to improve the livability of your home or are you doing it to make room for more stuff?[2]

The first step in assessing your true requirements is to introduce yourself to the concept that each of us only occupies about ten square feet or one square meter at a time. Apart from outright storage such as closets and cupboards, the rest of our space is visual (which we will cover in Chapter 5) or potential space.

We like to refer to the potential space phenomenon as the "bistro effect." You see them everywhere. A tiny wrought iron table flanked by two painfully uncomfortable wrought iron chairs. They pop up on lawns, patios, balconies, and in exquisitely landscaped flower gardens. They evoke visions of a café in Paris, accordion music accompanied by the clinking of glasses, or deep romantic stares into the eyes of a lover — except that no one ever actually sits in them.

This bistro effect is manifest in countless ways in our lives and has huge environmental consequences. If you think the embodied footprint of the humble nail is worth considering, imagine the carbon footprint of unused wrought iron furniture? There are countless examples such as the sailboat that languishes at the marina because we are too busy to use it, the sports car with flat tires in the garage, and the NordicTrack collecting dust in the attic.

The bistro effect is not just about stuff; it can also apply to function. Dedicating a section of the house to potential activities that you seldom if ever engage in is, from an environmental perspective, silly. Why not transform your living space into something that is fully functional, fully utilized, and fully enjoyed by you and your family on a day-to-day basis?

To do this with your renovation project you need to be prepared to step outside the norm of established design practices, if only temporarily, and explore the functionality of your current living space. Exercise 1 at the end of this section (also included within the download kit) will help you to assess where you actually live. It encourages you to log the frequency and time you spend in the various areas of your home. The results might surprise you. Especially if you take the data and use it to draw up a hypothetical floor plan that allocates the relative space of the kitchen, dining room, living room, den, etc., in proportion to the time they are actually used. Chances are that the proportionality of your space usage is currently quite different.

Another area worth exploring is whether your current living pattern reflects your personal values and the real values of your family

2 The Story of Stuff Project, accessed September 2014. http://storyofstuff.org/

or whether it is influenced by the design priorities of an architect long forgotten? For example, if you think you are watching too much TV, should this entertainment magnet, which actually draws your consciousness away from your home, be the center of your living space? Alternatively, if immersing yourself into the life experience of others through reality shows, movies, and documentaries is at the core of your family values, do you need to allocate space for a library or workout room? In that case maybe an elaborate home theater should be a top priority. The design of your home should, as much as possible, reflect what matters to you.

While every individual, every family, and every situation is unique, there are many common patterns of living that we share. For example, most of us spend way more time in the bathroom than the usually small spaces allocated to these rooms reflect. Dining rooms often turn into quasi-offices or work spaces that are not actually suited to the task. Kitchens still have that utilitarian feel but for the most part do not accommodate or enchant our daily routines.

We learned much about this from our sailboat. It's fun to play "live aboard" during our summer jaunts because it reminds us of when we were children and made cozy forts out of boxes and blankets. Instinctively we paid more attention to our human scale and how our space made us feel than the dictates of style and custom that dominate our adult minds now.

There is a principle that sailors who live on their boats employ. Everything on board has to have two purposes. Many of us view effective multitasking as a skill worth emulating and developing, but what about multitasking our rooms, spaces, and furniture? This may not be as difficult as it sounds. In fact, we already do it in many circumstances. The Murphy bed is a classic example. Another example may be your kitchen, where much of the space is probably occupied for different reasons at different times. Consciously tuning in to this strategy is a powerful design tool that can help spaces seem larger than they actually are.

1. Maximize the Space in Your Bathroom

Placing a stacked, front-loading washer and dryer into an upstairs bathroom is very practical indeed. After all, most of our laundry originates here. Another associated function that could be included in this space is an ironing board or sewing station that makes touch-ups or repairs to an evening dress or shirt a snap. Since these chores are seldom performed while taking a shower, curling your hair, or shaving,

Exercise 1
Room Use

Name of room: _____

What purpose does this room serve? _____

How many times a month do you think you use it? _____

This exercise will help you to determine how much time you spend in each room and if the rooms are used for other activities than those for which they are designed. After completing the exercise, you may decide some rooms need to be renovated to serve other activities if they are not being fully utilized in their current condition.

Using the form in the download kit, make a copy of the form for each room. For one month, keep a copy in each room and keep track of how many times a day you use each room. Also keep track of how long you were in the rooms and what activities you were doing.

At the end of the month, review each room's notes. Consider the following questions when evaluating each room:

1. Did you spend more or less time than you thought you would in this room?

2. Were there other purposes that the room served?

3. Were you surprised at any of your findings?

4. Does this room serve its purpose adequately?

5. Could you rearrange it to make it more functional?

6. Do you have to renovate it to make it more functional?

On a separate sheet of paper, make a list detailing what you like about each room and then create a list of what you dislike about each room. List the ways that you could renovate or change the dynamics of your rooms to improve the livability of your home.

Exercise 1 — Continued

Mon	Tue	Wed	Thu	Fri	Sat	Sun

Additional notes:

the floor space that is required to accommodate them can be shared with the floor space dedicated to the vanity and shower entrance. The net result is that the bathroom becomes a much larger living space that is utilized more frequently. So why is this not common practice?

One of the main challenges in sharing the bathroom with other activities is the generation of steam while taking a shower. Most shower enclosures are open at the top and there is a new trend emerging of walk-in shower stalls that replace the shower door with a short maze to protect the bathroom floor from secondary spray. These designs are inherent energy wasters on a number of fronts.

First, they require much more space to implement. An L-shape or maze design is inherently larger than a standard shower stall and we know that more space means more embodied energy and a larger carbon footprint. Second, they are cold since the warm moist air can easily escape and be replaced with relatively cool air from the room at large. This often results in hotter and longer showers that require more energy and water resources than necessary. Third, they fill the entire bathroom with a high humidity cloud of water vapor. This requires a large quantity of air to be expelled from the building to prevent the growth of mold and mildew.

Again, much of this design has its roots in the legacy of past practices. Traditionally showers have been lined with tiles surrounded by relatively porous grout. Tiled shower floors have long been constructed with two layers of deck mud that sandwich a rubber membrane. The result is that the deck mud above the rubber membrane and much of the grout will become waterlogged over time.

Since this makes it much harder for the shower to dry out between uses, the common remedy has been to allow the steam to escape the shower stall as quickly as possible. The consequences are fogged mirrors and condensation on the inside of windows and window frames. To combat this, the fan that is usually installed in the middle of the bathroom now needs to remove all the super-charged air from the entire space. Since that air is warm air that has to be made up with cold air from outside in the winter, the tendency is to make bathrooms small and confined living spaces.

This pattern is often repeated in house design. One problem gives rise to a solution that brings forth another problem that requires a solution which brings forth yet another problem and so on. The bathroom offers a perfect example of how this cycle of waste can easily be broken. Instead of applying fixes in layers, we need to meet the underlying challenge first.

By using fully molded plastic shower enclosures and the wonderful technology of KERDI mats employed by Schluter Systems we can create an effective water barrier as close to the surface of the shower as possible. As a result, the shower stall, whether molded fiberglass or tile, can much more readily dry between uses. This then allows us to fully enclose the shower stall so that the steam we generate during those blissful moments of immersion is retained and does not escape to the bathroom as a whole. A powerful exhaust fan mounted inside the shower stall can expel the moist air directly or, if you prefer a steam bath, be turned on after the shower is complete to quickly remove the water vapor.

Making the shower big enough to hang a towel in one corner to keep it dry completes this luxurious experience. The temperature in the shower stall will easily be ten degrees warmer than the room temperature, but since you have a chance to towel dry before stepping outside you don't feel the cooling effect of evaporation on your skin. No more mold on the ceiling, no more fogged mirrors, no more condensation on window frames, and no more wasted energy.

Now you are ready to explore new design ideas to turn your bathroom from a small, cramped utility room into a spacious living area that could even be open to the rest of the house. If a maze effect is to be employed, why not utilize it here to protect your privacy while allowing for the extravagant sight lines we will explore later. The toilet can always be segregated in an old-fashioned water closet if that is deemed necessary.

If we can successfully apply this concept to the bathroom, why not carry it through the rest of the house?

2. Make Your Bedroom Multipurpose

Most people spend less than an hour or two of their waking day in the bedroom. Either the bedrooms are small, dark, and often forgotten spaces somewhere at the back of the house, or they are opulent palatial expanses of largely unused, or at the very least, underutilized, energy hogging space. Most home designs try to find some middle ground, a compromise, along the spectrum between these two extremes. Why not take a new approach?

Using the principle of shared space we outlined for the bathroom in section 1., why not build your favorite activity into your bedroom? Maybe it's a workout room that reminds you to spend ten minutes before retiring to bed to do a few curls or sit-ups to keep in shape. Maybe it's an office so that when your muse speaks to you in that twilight of consciousness as you come awake, you can quickly record your inspiration before snuggling back between the covers for just ten more minutes. Maybe it's a sunroom that invites the morning rays to stream in from the east, or a place for stargazing as you drift off to sleep.

In our 14-by-36 foot, open-concept, multiuse second story, we incorporated these concepts of a modern master bedroom with en suite bathroom to create a fully functional and diversely attractive living space that is utilized for much of the day. By adding a balcony, we created an outside dimension that allows for sunrise meditations, blue sky study sessions, and night sky International Space Station watching in our pajamas.

3. Utilize the Space in Your Living Room and Dining Room

Let's take a closer look at what is likely the second most underutilized living space of your home — the living room and/or dining room. Yes, you may spend a lot of time there but chances are it's mostly to watch TV. The dining room, if used at all, usually serves as a rather inadequate, makeshift office. While these spaces may not be unoccupied, they are inherently poorly suited for the tasks that we ask them to perform.

The living room has its historical roots in the parlor of the nineteenth century where it was used to receive guests, host social events, and lay out the recently deceased before funerals. That is why to this day, many homes in North America still have front doors that open directly into this space.

In middle class homes, the living room tends to be a sort of catchall and as houses grow proportionally with the income bracket, they tend to become showpieces; an expression of style with chairs that are more comfortable for looking at than sitting.

No matter what our income bracket though, most of us have an intrinsic need for what in German is called "Geborgenheit." It's that sweet mix of comfort, safety, acceptance, love, warmth, and coziness that makes us seek the sun-drenched window bench or cushion-filled easy chair that swallows us whole. Standard living/dining room configurations have never evoked that feeling for us, so when we sought to create Geborgenheit in our main living space we looked for alternatives.

We found what we were looking for in Sarah Susanka's book, *The Not So Big House*, (The Taunton Press, 2008) while we were browsing through an old bookstore in the seaside town of Port Townsend. We had sailed there to attend the annual wooden boat festival. Sarah introduced us to the "inglenook," an old concept that we had never heard of before. Also known as the "chimney corner," the inglenook originated as a living space surrounding the hearth where people gathered to seek warmth by the fire. Part of a larger living space, it was often visually segregated by bench seating, or flanked with bookshelves. It sounded perfect.

Reading aloud to each other while swinging at anchor we knew we had stumbled onto an idea that would dramatically change the character and functionality of our home. Our decision to operate our home carbon-free precluded an actual fireplace but we loved the idea of creating a cozy nook in which to spend our long winter evenings. Instead of a real fireplace we adapted the concept to include an electronic fireplace and an electrically heated hearth. We reasoned that both could be run by solar energy in the future and give us a realistic effect. We decided to take a video of the firebox in the woodstove of our old house and play it in a loop on a surplus PC we had, leftover from the last round of upgrades.

Replacing the standard 12-by-18 foot living room we decided to drop the ceiling to 7 feet on a space of only 12-by-6 feet. With opposing bookshelves and bench seating at both ends it promised to be a gathering place that could comfortably accommodate four to six people. It also left room for a large, flat-panel video screen at one end, allowing the space to do double duty as a home theater. Knee walls at the foot of each bench segregated the space from the entry extension while keeping it within easy conversational reach of the expansive kitchen.

This was an especially important design consideration. To have a living space that is functionally independent and self-contained while at the same time easily integrated into the heart of the home during larger gatherings ensures its full and effective utilization. With only about seven feet separating the inglenook from the prep counter and its barstools at one end of the kitchen, lively conversation with guests remains fluid while the meal is being prepared. When hosting family reunions or neighborhood potlucks this multifunctional space transforms from an expansively extended foyer into a dining area that can accommodate folding tables and seat a dozen people comfortably.

4. Make Your Kitchen Welcoming to Visitors

Food has always been the glue that binds communities together. It is the focus of all our cultural, religious, and family gatherings. Preparing and sharing food is therefore the natural nucleus of any home. When we talked about the perfect design for our kitchen we found ourselves recalling again and again the ubiquitous scene played out in the sitcoms of our childhood. A friend or neighbor stops by unannounced, reaches over the Dutch door to turn the knob from the inside, and lets himself or herself in. The person heads for the fridge, pours a glass of milk, and gets comfortable at the kitchen table where he or she waits patiently to be discovered so he or she can share the news of their latest adventure.

While such scenes are rare in today's high-paced, wired world, when we host a gathering the underlying familiarity that it represents often emerges. Invariably, no matter how hard the host tries to steer things the other way, most of the liveliest conversations at any party take place in the kitchen. Food is sensual, it's personal, and it's intimate. It stands to reason that the place where our food is prepared is also the place where we drop all pretense and share of ourselves more openly with friends and family.

By exploring and recognizing this deep-rooted behavioral pattern we were able to abandon the idea of a dining room altogether. Instead we opted for a small 5-by-7 foot kitchen nook with bench seating that allows for seamless and casual interaction between the hosts and guests. In this case we didn't drop the ceiling. We wanted to highlight the glulam beams and Douglas fir planking of our vaulted ceiling.

So instead, we milled a broad beam from which hangs our retractable lamp and from where we also string our peppermint and garlic to dry.

Laura had her heart set on a Dutch door from the start. While we were still framing she found one in an online classified ad for $50. When we got it home I asked her where she wanted to store it and she looked at me dumbfounded. She didn't want to store it, she wanted to hang it! So without frame or jam and with a couple of old hinges we temporarily screwed it to the studs that lined the door opening.

Since then a hand-crafted, Douglas fir door jam and extra tough threshold milled from reclaimed Douglas fir planking have given our Dutch door a permanent hangout. We smile with satisfaction when a familiar "Hello" echoes through our house announcing the arrival of our neighbor Brent, who drops by with fresh cucumbers or blueberries from his garden and news about his puppy.

A welcoming kitchen not only serves as the centerpiece of a well-designed home but it can also act as a focal point for your immediate community. This is especially important when you have kids in the house; even for empty nesters it tends to enrich our lives in ways that are often overlooked in an insular world.

Of course, each house is different and so are the needs of its occupants. However, these green building concepts can be applied across a broad spectrum of circumstances. Apart from any other consideration, the mere fact that the space is minimized and used efficiently reduces both its embodied and operational carbon footprints. In our case, we were able to create a dynamic living space that easily fulfilled the role of living room, dining room, and kitchen in only 325 square feet.

5. Share Living Space

There is another way to renovate that reduces the carbon footprint while increasing the size of the living space. You can reduce the square footage of house per person by exploring creative ways of sharing your world. This can take many forms from cohousing to granny suites but they all start from the same premise: Not all living space has to be private. Your first reaction to this idea might be "No way! I don't want to live with strangers or in-laws." However, the benefits often outweigh the challenges by such a huge margin that considering a modernized approach to this age-old concept might be worth your while.

More and more jurisdictions are waking up to the notion that higher density housing, properly designed and carefully executed, creates a win-win scenario for home owners, municipalities, and the environment. It reduces urban sprawl and the paving over of valuable farmland; reunites families; allows seniors to live independently; supports mass transit and living streets; and builds vibrant neighborhoods by offering affordable housing for young couples and seniors alike.

A granny suite can be designed to nestle cozily into your home. It can serve as a luxurious guestroom, a flat for that 20-something offspring who is still searching for the right career, or private accommodation for a parent or senior who can maintain independence knowing that in an emergency help is close by.

Carriage houses or laneway houses are another alternative. They are officially known as Accessory Dwelling Units (ADUs). Check with your municipality if these are part of their master plan. Well designed, they offer the opportunity to reduce the total carbon footprint by utilizing space and resources more effectively. Any rent generated can also help to offset the cost of your eco-renovation and they provide an excellent alternative to the impersonal high-rise for seniors and young professionals.

Another approach you might want to explore is the concept of cohousing. You can connect with the Cohousing Association of the United States (www.cohousing.org) or the Canadian Cohousing Network (www.cohousing.ca) to see how you could adapt this concept to your situation. You don't need to move into an intentional community. You can apply some of the strategies in your own neighborhood. Simply organizing a common workshop or a community garden can improve the security of your neighborhood by building a sense of community.

Recently we met Linda who shared her family's firsthand experience in an article entitled "Sharing Homes & Hearts"[3]. Linda and her husband invited her parents to join their family in 1995 to share their 1,800-square-foot raised bungalow. The adventure was not without its challenges, but strategies for coexistence were developed and the children learned to be respectful of their older neighbors. "The energy and life in the house kept my parents young," Linda writes, "and their sense of responsibility, work ethic, and confidence along with a willingness to grow old with grace, inspired our children and gave them a sense of what senior living is all about." It was truly heartwarming to hear firsthand how it brought the generations together to build mutual trust and respect. But it also created other learning opportunities as knowledge and wisdom was shared across the generational divide. As the family aged their needs changed but this new living arrangement continued to serve them well.

---

3 "Sharing Homes & Hearts," by Linda Hunt, *Senior Living Magazine*, accessed September 2014. http://issuu.com/barbara.risto/docs/senior_living_feb13_final_web/60

There are many options that can be explored. Parents might choose to build a suite above a garage and accessible from the back alley for their newlywed son or daughter, with plans to rent it to a caregiver once the kids need bigger quarters to house children of their own. Or, an aging couple might choose to build a laneway house together so that should one predecease the other they can rent the main house, while remaining in the enchanted cottage built with their love in the backyard.

Every circumstance is unique and it doesn't always have to be done for family. There are opportunities to build long-lasting friendships across generations. When you have chosen the right community for your sustainable lifestyle, it makes sense to plan long term. But even if you move again, a home that is ready to accommodate the needs of an aging population will always find a ready market.

6. Consider Zoning Bylaws and Building Codes When Renovating

Zoning bylaws and building codes are in place to protect us from each other and ourselves. They should prevent shoddy workmanship, poor design, and dangerous circumstances. They should not prevent us from doing the right thing. Many municipalities have highly trained staff that is keen to move their communities into the twenty-first century. An application for a variance to build more sustainably will be welcomed in these jurisdictions. Only by demonstrating that there is a demand for new approaches can old rules be changed.

Before you renovate, check with your local municipal officials. You may be fortunate enough to already live in a community that encourages this forward-thinking approach. If not, remember that throughout our history, humans have voted with their feet. We have migrated to areas that allowed us to unfold our dreams and in so doing have created new communities with different characters. Why not give your property tax dollars to a municipality that understands sustainability issues. Your desire to live green can reach beyond your walls, into your yard, and through your community. See Exercise 2 at the end of this section to assess the livability of your community.

There are a growing number of contractors and designers that can help you materialize your family ideals. Urban Lanehomes[4] and Smallworks[5] are two of Vancouver's premier laneway house builders, and leaders in this field. You can draw inspiration from their modern designs.

4 Urban Lanehomes, accessed September 2014. http://www.urbanlanehomes.com
5 Smallworks, accessed September 2014. http://www.smallworks.ca

You might also look to examples in your region that help to build that small-town sense of community in a modern setting. You might find them in the older sections of town, closer to cultural events and sustainable transportation options such as bike paths and bus routes. You might find them in eco-village developments or senior cohousing units that help community elders to age in place. Or you might decide to lead by example and renovate your large house into a semi-duplex with a common kitchen and a community garden that allows you to share costs and resources while looking out for one another.

Of course there is a simpler way of reducing the carbon footprint of your renovation, and that is to not do it at all and simply prolong the life of what you already have by diligently keeping up with the maintenance. While this book will likely save you money in that approach too, you probably have already determined it's time to breathe new life into your home. In Chapter 3 we will explore the motivation that may lie behind that decision.

Exercise 2
Livability of Your Community

If you enjoy your neighborhood and community, you'll want to stay right where you are and adapt your present home to meet your needs. Take a good look at your neighborhood and community and then answer the following questions:

1. What do you like about this community?

2. What do you love about this community?

3. What do you dislike, but can live with, about this community?

4. What do you strongly dislike about this community?

5. Is this a municipality that you want to support with your tax dollars?

Yes	No	Look for the Things You Want in a Community
		Neighborhood feels safe.
Access to places that are important to you:		
		Shopping places nearby.
		Great restaurants.

		Neat coffee shops.
		Library.
		Cultural events (e.g., theater).
		Community center.
		Community events.
		Hospital.
		Recreation center.
		Doctor.
		Dentist.
		Specialists.
Access to places without having to use a vehicle:		
		Good public transportation.
		Good walking and bike paths.
		Close to your work.
		Close to the grocery store.
		Close to friends and/or family.
		Great hiking destination.
		Close to your children's schools.
		Close to major transportation hubs (e.g., airport, ferry, train, subway).

Additional notes:

3
Building for Resale or for Yourself

"I always wondered why somebody doesn't do something about that. Then I realized I was somebody."

— Lily Tomlin, Actress

In the early 1990s I attended a house building course taught by Harry Pasternak[1] of the Thousand Island Institute in Kingston, Ontario. The barn had a large renovated loft with four rows of stacking tables behind which we sat while listening to Harry's presentation. Over the course of a week we covered all aspects of building our own homes, from site selection to drywalling. We also spent a fair amount of time in the farmyard with hands-on mock-ups of framing and tiling.

Perhaps the two most valuable takeaways from this course were a mantra he repeated at the beginning of each class which we will cover in Chapter 9, and an exercise that we have adapted and would like to share with you now. Close your eyes. OK, open them again so you can read this but pretend you are closing your eyes.

---

1 Usable Makeover, Harry Pasternak, accessed September 2014.
http://www.usablemakeover.com/pasternak.html

Visualize yourself returning home from work on the most challenging and troubling day you can imagine. Everything went wrong. Now you are turning up your street and in a moment you will see it — your home. You can already feel the muscles in your shoulders relax as a smile slowly materializes on your face. You turn into your driveway and your sanctuary appears, inviting, welcoming, and comforting. You stop, breathe a huge sigh of relief, and walk through the front door.

Everywhere we go we are judged, scrutinized, and categorized. We wear suits, uniforms, makeup, and hairdos; props on the stage of life. All too often the character we play on that stage, our persona, doesn't adequately reflect the rich complexity of our inner being. It is created through necessity, or habit, or simply dictated by the career path we have chosen.

Our home may be the only place where we can find true expression of our ideals. It can be a canvas that unleashes our creativity. It can be a comfort zone where we find acceptance of our naked self. The way we furnish it, care for it, clean it, and organize it, already tells the world a lot about who we are. It reveals our priorities, our procrastination, and even our paranoia. But does it reveal our hidden potential? Does it inspire us to be the best that we can be? Does it evoke a sense of self confidence and strength that allows us to face Monday mornings with gusto? See Exercise 3 to help you evaluate the livability of your home.

Compromise is a process where we take two ideals and ask each to give up part of its perfection to accommodate the other. Sometimes compromise is worth the price it extracts from us, like when it prevents a conflict from escalating into war or when it facilitates the peaceful coexistence between two neighbors. However, compromise by definition does not breed excellence or perfection.

1. The Split-Level Home

A split-level house is a good example of compromise in home design that sacrifices the benefits of a ground-floor dwelling and a two-story home. It prevents the accessibility and intimacy with the garden that a single-story house can achieve and it offers none of the escalated views, balconies, and light manipulations that a second story can provide. It was made popular in the middle of the last century when suburbs experienced explosive growth after the Second World War.

In this century, when we see demographics changing with the aging of the baby boomers, the split level is perhaps the least appropriate housing configuration imaginable. Completely inaccessible to seniors relying on walkers or wheelchairs, it also offers little practicality to

Exercise 3
Livability of Your Home

This exercise will help you to determine if your home can be renovated to suit your needs. If so, it will help you to build on the strengths of your home and create a unique and remarkable indoor living space.

Take a good look at the interior of your house and then answer the following questions:

1. What do you like about this house?

2. What do you love about this house?

3. What do you dislike, but can live with, about this house?

4. What do you strongly dislike about this house?

5. Review your findings to determine the livability of your home: Can it be renovated to suit your needs? If so, list the ways that you could change the dynamics of your living space to improve the livability of your home.

the urban farmer of the twenty-first century, and makes it all but impossible to create a granny suite or guest suite with its own outside entrance, unless of course that suite is in the basement.

The second story also suffers since the addition of a balcony off a bedroom or a two-story atrium becomes difficult or impossible to execute. The location of the stairwell is often fixed to the location of the front door, resulting in forced floor plans that lack creativity and functionality. These result in unnecessarily larger houses, accompanied by their increased carbon footprint.

The one place where a split level, if designed properly, can work extremely well is if the home is positioned on a sloping lot. In this case it can allow direct ground-level accessibility on two sides while maintaining the natural grade of the lot. Depending on lot size this can be accomplished by orienting the home or addition in line with the slope of the grade rather than the surveyed property lines.

Most often though, that is not where the split level is found. Instead it fills flat subdivisions all over the country with functionally challenged structures that are showing their age. They are not the only compromised layout that has left a legacy which is difficult to sustain. Even today, many commercial builders and developers are opting for townhouse designs that include massive, complex, and extremely wasteful roof structures over sprawling homes with minimal garden space.

The interior is still comprised of a standard living room, dining room, and three-bedroom layout with the concession to our aging population of a main floor bedroom that has an en suite bathroom. Ironically, the master bedroom and master bathroom are usually still upstairs making this design inconvenient if not impractical when it comes time to accommodate a live-in caregiver.

The reason most developers choose this design is that it offers a compromise. Most home buyers can see some of their needs met if not perfectly, then at least partially. Since there are no affordable alternatives (most of us cannot justify the expense of a custom-built home), the general public has adopted an attitude of resigned acceptance. Perfection remains elusive and seemingly out of reach.

Statistics show, on average, American home owners sell and move every five to seven years. According to the US Census Bureau, if you take away the need to move for a new job or transfer, in 2008/2009 the main reason for moving was to find a better, more livable home. Many of these moves took place within the same county; that is, they were driven by a need to change the functionality of the home and not necessarily its location.[2]

2. Staying Put in an Ideal Location

When we consider that listing and closing fees can range between 3 and 5 percent of the home purchase price and the average Canadian home hovers around $400,000,[3] we can calculate that moving this often can translate into $4,000 per year in transaction costs alone. If you like your neighborhood and are well situated vis-á-vis bus routes, bike paths, and other sustainable transportation options, it makes good economic sense to stay put and build your green legacy right where you are.

We mention these considerations here because right on the heels of the carbon footprint of our homes is the carbon footprint of our transportation choices. To be truly sustainable we should integrate the two into a lifestyle that not only improves our heath and quality

2 "Why People Move: A Deeper Look at the Data," Arun Barman, *Economists' Outlook*, accessed September 2014. http://economistsoutlook.blogs.realtor.org/2011/03/02/why-people-move-a-deeper-look-at-the-data/
3 "Canadian House Prices," Living in Canada, accessed September 2014. http://www.livingin-canada.com/house-prices-canada.html

of life, but also makes us feel proud of our accomplishments. Therefore, any strategy to green your home should also take into account
and facilitate the most effective way that we can reduce our carbon
footprint — to get out of our vehicles.

3. Resale Value

Let's assume you are ready to convert your home from a place to sleep
and watch TV to a sanctuary for you and your loved ones. How important is it to renovate for the marketplace? Should you really listen to
all those voices that tell you to build to the lowest common denomina-
tor so that your home has resale value?

Let's begin by splitting the value of your property into its two components: land and building. The value of the land rises and sometimes
falls with its location. Easy access to transportation and other ameni-
ties will allow your land value to rise. Assuming you have decided to
stay where you are, the rate of this rise is largely beyond your control.

There is one caveat we should mention here. If you renovate with
zest and imagination, you may well set new standards for your neighborhood. Other home owners on your street may draw courage from
your initiative and undertake their own eco-renovations. This could
result in a general community upgrade over time which will, naturally, translate into increased property values.

Where you do have a lot of latitude and control is in the building side of the equation. Will your renovation add resale value to your
home? The standard approach tends to be to emulate the style and concepts currently employed by local developers. Remember these styles
change and so a house and even a whole neighborhood can easily become dated. It takes a long time for a tract home to become a classic.

With this approach, the argument goes, you will build to suit a
large cross section of the population and hence be assured of a quick
sale when you decide to move, yet again. This approach is usually
championed by the real estate community which has a vested interest
in your endless search for "just the right place to live," and the developers who know that they can easily outcompete a renovation with
new construction if both look and feel essentially the same.

The alternative perspective, one we would like to explore in more
detail here since the other side is already well represented, is to build
on the strengths of your home and create a unique and remarkable living space that stands out in the crowd; something that not only meets
your needs perfectly but can do the same for buyers who just can't

find a property to match their modern lifestyle. You will never sell your home to the "average" home buyer because that person doesn't exist. Few of us like to think of ourselves as average, and in the end it only takes one family who falls in love with your vision to make a sale.

How much latitude does this perspective give you? Quite a lot, but maybe not as much as you fear. The main reason most people shy away from this second approach is the plethora of opinions that seek to dissuade innovation. No doubt they will continue to influence your decisions no matter how much you seek to express your creativity. This peer pressure will probably prevent you from going too far but hopefully not from going far enough.

What we recommend is to put all that aside and start by visualizing the perfect home for you and your family. Then, plan a renovation to upgrade your existing home towards that ideal as far as your budget allows. At the end of this process, it will be soon enough to consider the marketability of your dream. In fact, the results might surprise you. If you incorporate the latest design concepts for sustainable lifestyles as part of your vision, you will build a home suited to the twenty-first century.

4. Think outside the Box

Let's explore a few ideas that can help you think outside the box. These ideas could improve the livability of your home, extend its functional lifespan, and reduce the operating costs and associated carbon footprint. They are not meant as recommendations because they might not suit your purpose or family circumstance. They are simply meant as illustrations to get the ideas flowing.

The most efficient shape for a dwelling made from modern building materials is a square box preferably with dimensions that are easily divided into the standard sizes of sheathing or cladding. Of course, flat roofs are hard to keep water tight and square boxes lack that certain *joie de vivre*. To minimize the cost per square foot of your home it is a shape that pops up again and again, albeit in a slightly modified form.

When building or renovating sustainably, a common question you will be asked is "What did it cost per square foot?" It's a question that sounds legitimate enough until you explore its meaning in a little more depth. Bathrooms and kitchens are very expensive to build and renovate. More than half the electrical circuits in your home will serve your kitchen and most of the plumbing will originate in the bathroom.

Since every modern home will likely have one kitchen and two bathrooms, the smaller the home, the larger the percentage of total construction cost incurred by these two rooms. The result is that to reduce the cost per foot it's best to build a 10,000-square-foot home with a small kitchen and two small bathrooms; hardly a recipe to boost its resale potential or livability, let alone reduce its carbon footprint.

Buying a home based on its cost per square foot is akin to buying a dress based on its cost per square inch or a vehicle based on its cost per pound. When renovating or building sustainably, you should look beyond this simple measure and keep your eyes firmly fixed on the prize; an efficient home that reflects your values and offers you sanctuary. Let's look at a couple of examples.

The atrium is one concept that could be included in a renovation. It does not have to be grand in style but can simply replace a typical dormer in an old-fashioned roof line. Turning the dormer into a second story sunroom could create an inside balcony that would provide passive solar gain in the spring, increased access to sunlight in the winter, and if opened to the first floor, a chimney-effect that could help cool the house in summer. The latter may seem a little counter intuitive but as you'll see in Chapter 5, it can work quite well.

While on the roof, you should explore common roof lines and their origins. Early dwellings and small structures often have what is commonly called a "shed roof." Also known as a mono-pitched roof, this design retains many advantages over the more common gable roof or hipped roof so often employed today. Mono-pitched roofs are considerably more resilient in earthquakes since they usually transmit all loading downward, and can withstand hurricane winds more effectively because they do not create an airfoil shape that can actually create lift.

It is likely that we migrated from shed roofs to gabled roofs to accommodate larger dwellings with the limited span capacity of the timbers employed at the time. Of course, modern lamination techniques, glulam beams, and advanced truss designs have long ago overcome this obstacle but we still tend to build more complex interlocking roof structures based on the traditional gable or hip roof. Not only are these more expensive to install and maintain, but they also severely restrict the ability to mount solar panels as you will see in Chapter 8.

They also tend to result in a huge amount of wasted real estate and can become a heat trap that can make even a well-insulated home quite uncomfortable in the summer. Seldom are these roofs adequately ventilated and what little ventilation they have is often disturbed and sometimes eliminated by the installation of added insulation. Most of these roof designs do not offer any usable attic space and if the area under the roof is built out, it often results in code violations regarding headroom requirements. Shed roofs by comparison offer additional visual space which creates a sense of roominess and the possibility for usable lofts.

Enclosed courtyards, covered patios, and front porches are three more ways to change the dynamics of your living space and offer opportunity to improve the livability of your home. In addition to their positive impact on sightlines and maintenance challenges, which we will cover in subsequent chapters, they can be used to create centers of activity that benefit the whole family. (See Exercise 4 at the end of this chapter to analyze the livability of your property.)

For example, the covered front porch is a common feature of traditional homes built at the turn of the last century; this design element has been largely forgotten. Exploring the history, it is likely that front porches were often closed in to create extra internal living space and this enclosed space was then gradually assimilated into the envelope of the home. In the process many of the benefits of a front porch were lost.

There was a time when the "neighborhood watch program" consisted of Grandpa sitting in his rocking chair on the front porch. Children were able to play unsupervised and the community was safe and secure. Actively used front porches contributed to more neighborhood communication and a higher sense of awareness of community activity. Everyone knew when the neighbors went away for the weekend and they looked out for strangers that might knock on their door.

This was a quieter, gentler time; we sought to recapture it with a covered front porch on our small-footprint home. We wanted the porch to mimic the design of the rest of the house and so found ourselves on a cold and blustery February day sorting through a lift of 4-by-8 Douglas fir beams at a local lumberyard. We put our hands on seven straight sticks that were suited to our post and beam design provided they would stay true during the curing process.

When we dug out the beams from our weighted drying pile a year later, one had warped, requiring us to replace the ridge beam with a one-inch board. Much sanding and love was needed to turn the blackened beams into the radiant golden timbers that earned the right to be called "functional art." We simulated fir roof-decking by ripping fir plywood into plank-sized strips and beveling the edges to mimic the look of tongue and groove. We matched the green metal roofing of the house and temporarily furnished it with benches (until we find the time to complete our built-ins).

The porch is flanked by juniper bushes, scarlet rhododendrons, and ferns, all native to the area. The blossoms of the plum tree send their fragrance drifting across its occupants in the spring, and the summer sun bathes it in warmth during breakfast even though it faces north. It has become a place where we enjoy many meals and much lively conversation as we keep an eye on one neighbor's bamboo and another neighbor's potatoes. Folks walking their dogs or riding their bikes offer a friendly wave and friends are readily welcomed as they drop in for a glass of iced tea on a hot summer's evening.

Not only has it created another living space in which we can entertain guests but it encouraged us to create a wooded enclave, a fruit orchard, a berry patch, and a vegetable garden plot that bring joy to Maria, the newspaper lady, Fred the postman, and Sarah the water-meter reader. Last summer we added a glass table and four steel chairs we found at a garage sale, to facilitate "front yard dining" in our "inglenook garden"; the bistro effect in reverse.

Our porch has truly transformed our front yard from a buttress against the "dangerous outside world" into an active and vibrant living space that has made it possible to feel comfortable with a glass front door. By forging a direct link between us and our community this simple design concept has truly changed the dynamic of our lives.

The front porch is but one example of how innovation can adapt the successful strategies of the past with a modern desire to rebuild community and improve our way of life in the twenty-first century. Growing food on our urban lot and sharing the surplus with our neighbors is another. By creating centers of activity that are tuned to whatever your passion might be, you are not only adding character to your home but adding value to your life.

Many of these centers of activity don't have to be confined to your main house, they can be garden studios or workshops, outdoor eating terraces or summer kitchens. Protected balconies can even harness a microclimate for sunbathing in the buff or other extravagant lifestyle activities. By actively using outside space as part of your living experience you are reconnecting with the seasons and the very essence of what sustainable building practices are trying to preserve.

In the next chapter we will explore how you can build or renovate to last. No matter how you choose to proceed, your renovation will inevitably leave a legacy and have an impact on your neighborhood. Building functional art that is environmentally sustainable not only benefits your family today but it can enrich future generations that will appreciate your courage and willingness to pay it forward.

Exercise 4
Livability of Your Property

This exercise will help you to determine if your property can be renovated to suit your needs. If so, it will help you to build on the strengths of your property and create unique and remarkable outdoor living spaces.

Take a good look at the exterior of your house and property and then answer the following questions:

1. What do you like about the property?

2. What do you love about the property?

3. What do you dislike, but can live with, about the property?

4. What do you strongly dislike about the property?

5. Review your findings to determine the livability of your property: Can it be renovated to suit your needs? If so, list the ways that you could change the dynamics to improve the livability of your property.

4
Building to Last: Key Maintenance Issues

"The first rule of sustainability is to align with natural forces, or at least not try to defy them."

— Paul Hawken, Environmentalist, Entrepreneur, and Author

There is a rule of thumb we adopted when building our small-footprint home that has served us well. Anything made of wood should last as long as it took the trees to grow. Of course, it's mostly a hypothetical yardstick because it's challenging to figure out exactly how long a tree had to grow to allow us to mill a two-by-six out of it, and clearly not everything in a house is made of wood, but it set us up with a way of thinking that focused on the longevity of all the products we used. As we have learned, the embodied carbon footprint of our home is greatly affected by how long it lasts and making good decisions in this regard is the green thing to do.

1. Exterior Materials

Why not build everything out of concrete and steel? In fact, if you look at industrial buildings and skyscrapers, that is mostly what happens. However, concrete, like steel, requires a huge amount of energy to produce and until we have converted fully to wind, solar, and hydro as our sources for electricity the carbon footprint is considerable. This carbon cost can be mitigated with steel roofing and siding as it can be easily returned to the mill as feedstock, but with concrete that is considerably more difficult. When it's recycled, it serves mostly as a replacement for gravel underlay since the production of new concrete requires the removal of all impurities through an elaborate washing process.

1.1 Stone

Concrete and steel, or more generally stone and metal do have the advantage that they are extremely durable when exposed to the elements and are practically maintenance free. The most durable and sustainable example of stone in construction is handed down to us from the Inca stonemasons who built dry stone structures at Cusco in Peru, now almost 1,000 years old. These employed no mortar and are breathtaking in their beauty, at least to anyone who has ever laid a brick. Our modern equivalent of river rock or field stone with mortar are no match for the ancient Incas but they are a great alternative to poured concrete where circumstances allow and time permits.

1.2 Rammed earth

Another amazing building technique that is being revived in many parts of the country is rammed-earth construction. It's an ancient technique that uses materials readily available. The "earth" can be comprised of clay, sand, and gravel, and can be stabilized with lime or chalk. Instead of pouring concrete into forms the earth is tamped in layers into similar forms that can be removed as soon as the wall is complete. Rammed-earth walls can be simple to construct, use local materials, create thermal mass, and are aesthetically very appealing with their stratified, multicolored layers of clay. They need dry conditions to last and are well-suited as a substitute for internal applications of stone because of their architectural appeal.

Rammed earth, stone, and concrete are also insect-proof and require little or no finishing; the exception being in places where water can seep into cracks and freeze. As a general rule, all matter tends to expand when heated and contract when cooled. It's a process we rely on often in our everyday lives and is what makes the lids on your mason jars go "pop" in the evening after you have spent an afternoon canning preserves in your kitchen.

Water also expands as it warms and contracts as it cools; that's why ocean warming contributes to sea level rise, but it does something very odd around the freezing mark. As water is cooled to the freezing point it contracts normally but once it reaches 39 degrees Fahrenheit (4 degrees Celsius) it reaches maximum density. Then as it continues to cool, it expands by as much as 9 percent. This is why icebergs float and why, thankfully, our oceans are not filled with solid ice. It is also why, in cold climates, stone walls crumble and why the Rocky Mountains will one day look like the Canadian Shield.

There are many ways to protect stone and mortar from this effect and all involve some sort of waterproofing. Overhangs and flashing can be used to keep the mortar dry and thereby contribute to its life span but the objective is always the same: You don't want water to find its way into tiny cracks where it can freeze. This will guarantee that your grandest design will turn into rubble over time.

2. Foundation

Now that we have considered stone above ground, let's take a closer look at foundations. The number one job of a foundation is to protect the house from the very effects of freezing water described above. When waterlogged soil freezes it expands with a force that can literally lift buildings.

The center of the earth is hot — really hot. In fact, it is molten iron with temperatures reaching more than 9,000 degrees Fahrenheit (5,000 degrees Celsius). That's why, even in the cold of winter, frost only penetrates a few feet in a temperate climate. Foundations are constructed so that the broad footer at the bottom, which distributes the load over a wider footprint, lies beneath the frost layer. It is at this level that we also find the perimeter drain which is discussed in section 3.

Concrete foundations are generally sealed from the outside with tar or the new, and much more effective peel-and-stick membranes. Until about 30 years ago, we had to rely on tar-based products that were usually sprayed or brushed onto the surface. These never waterproofed the foundations but rather damp-proofed them to keep out water vapor and reduce the capillary action of concrete. However, standing water against a foundation wall can easily overcome damp proofing and seep into your basement.

When building an addition or planning a renovation, it is wise to familiarize yourself with these details which may not be readily apparent in your home. A heaving foundation can ruin your new drywalling job and can make that perfectly hung door stick in the winter months. It is not just frost heaving you need to be concerned about. Even the swelling and shrinking of clay, as a result of water saturation and drying, can lift sections of the wall.

3. Perimeter Drain

More than any other detail of your home the proper functioning of your perimeter drain can extend the lifespan of your house and therefore reduce its carbon footprint over time. The concept is quite simple. A perforated pipe is placed at the level of your concrete footer and is connected to your storm sewer or on a sloping lot, and exits downhill. This perforated pipe (holes at the bottom) is covered in clean gravel which can extend all the way up to the surface. If you want to plant a flower garden next to your foundation, a layer of thick landscape cloth should be placed at the gravel-to-soil interface to provide extra protection from silt. It also helps to separate the soil from the cloth with a layer of sand. This is a little more arduous than just backfilling your drainpipe but it will ensure that your perimeter drain will function well for decades.

Placing the gravel all the way up, or almost all the way up the foundation wall, allows the water to drain easily. This has two benefits: Not only does it eliminate any hydrostatic pressure buildup during the rainy season but it also eliminates the risk of foundation damage due to ice pressure. Ice pressure is generated if the soil is saturated within the frost zone close to the surface and the foundation is well insulated. The frozen soil, as it expands, can exert enough pressure over time to crack concrete. This is especially true if no heat escapes from the basement as a result of an eco-friendly renovation that included a thick layer of insulation.

All this will not only keep your foundation in good shape but it will also keep your basement dry, which can allow you to add more living space to your home. A dry basement can house everything from a workshop to a wine cellar, from a media room to a pantry. Integrating the basement into your home's ventilation system will also allow you to exploit the naturally cooler temperatures of a dry basement without adding extra humidity to your envelope.

4. Condensation and the Building Envelope

The building envelope is the next most important consideration before you embark on your eco-renovation. The building envelope is comprised of the layers that keep the elements out and keep comfort in. Understanding the way your envelope works and the physics that act on it will help you determine the effectiveness of not only your current design but the implications for your renovation plans.

It's a Saturday afternoon in July. You are hosting a picnic in your backyard. The kids are jumping through the sprinkler while your friends and neighbors engage in lively conversation on your patio. You pour yourself a cold one and place it in front of you on the glass table. You take in the scene and count your blessings. Soon, you notice a puddle forming at the bottom of your glass as beads of water roll down its frosted stem. "My glass is leaking!" you think to yourself. As quickly as that thought flashes through your mind you dismiss it. Everyone else's glass is dripping too and you have seen this a hundred times before.

Of course, your glass wasn't leaking. What you saw was condensation in action. It's a common, if poorly understood, phenomenon that can be devastating to your home. Simply put, condensation occurs when there is more moisture in the air than the air can support and the moisture needs to precipitate out somehow. This is what causes rain, clouds, and fog to form. Pilots and sailors are well acquainted with this "dew point" and monitor weather forecasts regularly. However, most of us have never thought about considering the weather forecast inside our walls.

4.1 Relative humidity

To understand dew point, you need to understand the concept of relative humidity. Air has a finite capacity to carry moisture and that capacity fluctuates with temperature. The warmer the air, the more moisture it can carry in suspension. At -20 degrees Fahrenheit (-29 degrees Celsius) air can hold little or no moisture and is therefore very dry. By the time it reaches the melting point at 32 degrees Fahrenheit (0 degrees Celsius) 1,000 cubic feet of air can hold about one-third of a pound (almost 5 ounces) of water. At 68 degrees Fahrenheit (20 degrees Celsius), the optimum temperature for living spaces, that same 1,000 cubic feet of air can hold about one pound (16 ounces) of water and at 100 degrees Fahrenheit (38 degrees Celsius) it can hold almost three times that.

The relative humidity of air is the measure of saturation at a given temperature and not the actual amount of water present in a given volume of air. Since 1 pound of water is approximately 16 fluid ounces (depending on temperature), Table 1 shows the relative humidity at different temperatures and water concentrations for 1,000 cubic feet of air (roughly the size of an average bedroom that is 10-by-12-by-9 feet.

Table 1
Relative Humidity Chart

Temperature	Amount of Water	Carrying Capacity	Relative Humidity
10 °F (-12°C)	1.6 oz.	1.6 oz.	100%
32 °F (0 °C)	1.6 oz.	5 oz.	32%
68 °F (20 °C)	1.6 oz.	16 oz.	10%
80 °F (27 °C)	1.6 oz.	27 oz.	6%
100 °F (38 °C)	1.6 oz.	46 oz.	3%

It is generally accepted that the optimum relative humidity for human comfort is somewhere between 35 and 50 percent. As you can see, a well-ventilated home (or a very drafty one) can easily be too dry for comfort inside as the outside temperature drops in winter. That is why humidifiers were commonplace before people began to weather-strip and seal their homes.

Today the opposite tends to be true. Cooking, bathing, showering, and just breathing all add huge amounts of moisture into the air of our home. The average person in your household will release about two pounds (32 ounces) of moisture through respiration and transpiration each day. That can add up to a lot of moisture which needs to be vented. How this is best accomplished without losing the associated heat will be covered in Chapter 5. Suffice it to say that for the purpose of this discussion, you can assume that the relative humidity in a modern home will likely hover closer to the higher end of the comfort spectrum.

Let's assume that the relative humidity is at 50 percent during the winter with an indoor air temperature of about 68 degrees Fahrenheit (20 degrees Celsius). The actual amount of water in this hypothetical bedroom is about one-half pound (eight ounces). About the amount of liquid in that cold one you were enjoying on the patio before we filled your head with all this stuff!

Now let's assume this warm air, with its relatively normal moisture content, could travel freely through walls. As it grew colder, its capacity to hold moisture would drop and conversely its relative humidity would rise. When it reached about 45 degrees Fahrenheit (7 degrees Celsius), it would reach the saturation point of 100 percent relative humidity. This is called the dew point. As it cooled even further it would be forced to lose some of its moisture in the form of condensation. By the time it dropped to 10 degrees Fahrenheit (-12 degrees Celsius), an average temperature in Canadian winters, it would have to lose about one-third of a pound (5.4 ounces) of water and it would essentially be raining in the walls.

Clearly this would not be a good thing, since the accumulation of moisture in the outside walls not only renders the insulation ineffective but also triggers wood rot in alarmingly rapid progression. That is why modern building codes are becoming increasingly strict about the careful application of vapor barriers. These are generally placed on the inside of the framing members to keep the warm air in the fully heated space where it can easily keep its moisture content in suspension.

The challenge arises in maintaining the continuity of that barrier around floor joists and at the old-to-new transition points in renovations or additions. Each circumstance is different but if you keep the above-described principles in mind, and use them to recognize any location where warm air can potentially traverse into a cold space, you will be able to apply due diligence and avoid most moisture problems in your home. Don't forget that the same principle applies in your bathroom, shower stall, kitchen, and even to the warm, moist air of summer as it enters your air-conditioned home.

To illustrate how frequently you will encounter this phenomenon, let's step outside for a moment and take a look at the siding of our small-footprint home. For a variety of reasons we employed a rain-screen in our exterior envelope design which has the effect of creating a three-quarter-inch air gap between the siding and the home wrap/ air and water barrier-covered sheathing underneath.

The building code required that we vent this space by installing a bug screen at the bottom of each wall section but at the time it said nothing about venting the top. Since we anticipated that the sun hitting the HardiePlank® siding would naturally heat this space to higher than ambient temperatures, we knew that the actual moisture content of that super-heated air space could be elevated during the day. At night, when the air temperature dropped, as it does in our climate, the air would not be able to suspend all that moisture and it would likely condensate out against the back of the siding. In this case, a simple fix was to facilitate the natural convection currents by installing a bug screen at the top of each wall section as well. Now the air could circulate freely and thereby prevent any condensation.

As you can see calculating the location of the dew point in any circumstance can help you. It can also clarify why proper venting of exterior wall cavities is so critical. It can even help our understanding of the placement of wood components in design. Before we go there, we need to address one common trap that awaits us as we increase the insulation of our home in an eco-renovation: The double vapor barrier.

Some might assume that since one vapor barrier is good, two are better. Why not place a vapor barrier on the outside of the insulated stud cavity to protect against the humid days of summer and another on the inside to protect against the cold days of winter? Unfortunately, it's not that simple. While this concept does work in double-glazed windows, it is practically impossible to create the hermetically sealed conditions it demands in a wall cavity. You simply cannot control the humidity inside the wall that precisely, and some moisture will invariably be present. This moisture, firmly locked into place by two carefully applied vapor barriers, will rot out the bottom plates of your stud wall in short order.

This is important to keep in mind when adding extra insulation during your renovation. Recognize that your dew point will move as you do so; make sure that this does not change the dynamics of your envelope in detrimental ways. Be especially careful when mixing different types of insulation material. Sheet insulation is often impermeable to air and moisture and if sealed around the edges, forms an effective vapor barrier all by itself. Combining it with blown-in or fiberglass insulation requires careful consideration of the dew point, something you are now equipped to do.

4.2 R-value and P2000 insulation

R-value is a measure of thermal resistance. A standard exterior stick frame wall does not have a homogenous R-value. Although the building code dictates an R-value for exterior walls, this value is usually only achieved where insulation is present. In a two-by-six stud cavity, the R20 rating applies to the cavity only, the studs have a rating of around R6, and if there is a gap between the studs and the insulation, it can have no R-value at all. A heat-sensing gun, readily available and affordable, can help you easily locate these and other thermal bridges in your envelope.

Since interior envelope designs rely on ventilating the studs from the exterior, you cannot add exterior insulation in the form of panels without creating this double-vapor barrier effect. You can add a thin, radiant barrier such as three-eighths P2000 insulation between the studs and the drywall if your renovation includes drywall work on the inside of exterior walls. This material is much more effective than its three-eighth inch thickness would suggest since it primarily addresses itself to reflecting the radiant heat energy back into the room.

Modern construction techniques often use reflective insulation barriers such as P2000 in external envelopes that have the added benefit of keeping your framing timber inside, where it's always warm and dry. This approach can greatly extend the life of your home and has multiple benefits including warm windowsills. However, while used extensively in commercial construction, external envelopes are not yet the industry standard for residential homes. They are more complex and can be more costly to employ. If you choose to consider an external envelope for your renovation, pay special attention to the lateral support of your framing and the old/new transition to keep your vapor barrier contiguous.

4.3 Wood

As we already mentioned, the carbon footprint of any construction or renovation project is greatly impacted by how long the work stands up to natural deterioration.

Many people recognize that concrete and steel can last a long time with minimal maintenance; however, most prefer wood. Why? Because people have an affinity for wood. Wood is alive, vibrant, and real; we owe our civilization to its magical properties. Our relationship with wood goes back to the beginning of our species. It was our source of warmth and shelter for a long time. Eventually it facilitated the smelting of metals and building of ships. Wood was used as supports in early coal mines and the first oil derrick was constructed of it. Wood was used to build the first furniture and factories.

Is it any wonder that it evokes a feeling of comfort and security in our being? It is often preferred, even if only in its pictorial representations printed on laminate flooring or pressboard kitchen cabinets. Solid wood doors give a stately feel to the smallest cabin and wood floors are still the highest choice of excellence and durability. But all too often the dynamics of wood take a backseat to style, short-term cost considerations, and convenience.

Employed inside the building envelope where the temperature and humidity is relatively stable throughout the year, wood can last a lifetime with minimal maintenance. It is a classic with its natural colors that slowly morph into ever deeper and richer hues. Wood accumulates the patina that tells a story of days gone by. Wood is warm, durable, strong, and timeless.

It is when we try to capture that same feeling outside the building envelope that things get tricky. As you'll see in Chapter 5, the micro-climates around our home have distinct characteristics that change through the seasons. These affect all building materials but they can be especially detrimental to wood.

When wood is exposed to the elements, it is in its natural habitat. Wood in the forest either grows or decays and since your planking, siding, or window frames are no longer growing, they are keen to decay back into soil for the next generation of trees. In this they are aided by a variety of natural forces. Exposure to direct summer sun will dry the wood fiber. The extraction of moisture generally causes the exposed side of a plank to shrink, cup, and split. This offers opportunity for moisture to enter during the rainy season, which in turn invites fungus, ants, and beetles. You might even hear the alarm bells of a woodpecker's hammering as it tries to extract these little morsels with destructive exuberance.

In the shade, the process is more gradual. It is estimated that there are between 100,000 and 1 million species of fungi on the planet and many of them thrive in cool, damp spaces. They contribute to the natural forces of deterioration. This is especially true if they are exposed to the rain. Counteracting all these natural processes often requires fungicides and other poisons that certainly have no place in an eco-friendly home. It also requires a diligent and active maintenance schedule and if this is not maintained, early replacement of deteriorated wood beams, trim, and siding.

There is, however, a simple and effective way to protect exterior wood from this fate. Broad overhangs, well-designed porches, and covered patios can greatly increase the durable life of wood surfaces by protecting them from direct sunlight and rain. Our Dutch door, which was used before we had it, will likely last many decades more because it is under cover and out of the harm of any direct sunlight, tucked into the corner of a southeast facing, covered patio.

Our front door and its handcrafted, naturally finished, Douglas fir trim is equally protected under the north-facing porch. After five years, their beauty already stands in sharp contrast to the weathered exterior Douglas fir glulam beams on the eastern and western extremities of our main roof. Although they are under a slight overhang, these face the direct assault of the morning and evening sun as well as rain driven horizontally by winter storms.

Equally contrasting weathering patterns are evident in the wood combing that we mistakenly used to trim our windows and the corners of our fiber cement siding. We followed local building convention and employed the same combination of materials used by most professional builders in our area. Combing is basically cheap fir boards that are primed white, with a roughed up or "combed" surface that is purported to eliminate cracking and warping.

Although we were skeptical of this claim and secured the trim well to hold it firmly in place, it has become evident that the ravages of direct sunlight will cause exposed sections to crack and fail long before the flashing of our metal roof or the HardiePlanks that make up our siding.

The day will come when we have to strip this trim and tediously replace it; it will come much sooner than if we had matched the life cycle of the products for this application. In the meantime we are faced with increased maintenance.

The cost of erecting staging on a two-story home is the same whether you paint just the trim or paint the siding as well. As you can see, matching the maintenance and life cycles of adjoining components makes environmental and economic sense.

5. Annual Inspection and Maintenance Tasks

Now that you have a deeper understanding of the underlying issues, let's take a closer look at the annual inspections and maintenance tasks that will help to maximize the life span of your home and reduce its carbon footprint.

Make sure that your perimeter drain and rain leaders are functioning properly. (See Exercise 5.) Well-designed perimeter drains have easily accessible cleanouts that let you run a snake to check for obstructions such as built-up silt, tree roots, and gutter debris. This can be harder to do in older perimeter drains and you will have to rely on other clues. One simple test is to remove a gutter downspout and place your garden hose in its drain. If you can turn the water on full blast and not see the water backing up, your perimeter drain is either in good shape or you have just flooded the basement.

The next step is to carefully inspect for damp spots in your home. (See Exercise 6 at the end of this chapter.) Start in your crawl space or basement and look around the exterior walls where the floor joists rest on the sill plates. You will need a flashlight to do this. Pay special attention to areas underneath dishwashers, sinks, tubs, showers, and washing machines. If you find moisture, mold, or water stains, you need to explore further. Rule out the obvious first, such as leaking pipes, hoses, or fittings. Once these have been ruled out, check for possible leaks in the external cladding. Finally apply what you have learned about the dew point and look for any breaches in the vapor barrier.

If your basement has already been remodeled, this job is harder but you may still be able to find telltale signs of moisture. Remember that wallpaper will easily peel and blister on damp drywall, and mold that reappears, no matter how many times you wash it off with bleach, is a strong indicator of persistent moisture. This could be wicking out from a moist wall cavity behind the drywall, possibly containing wet insulation, or be condensing on cold surfaces caused by a thermal bridge.

Your next stop should be your attic. Again, cover the obvious first to see if there are any signs of a leaking roof. Fiberglass or blown-in insulation in conjunction with a plastic vapor barrier can hold and divert a lot of water before it becomes noticeable in your living space. If you catch this early, it can save you a lot of money and reduce the environmental and financial costs of remediation.

Once you have convinced yourself that your roof is not leaking, it's time to consider ventilation and condensation. It's hard to believe but there are still houses where the bathroom fans are simply vented into the attic cavity. Not only is this ineffective in actually venting your bathroom but it spells disaster for joists and rafters. Check to make sure that the piping of your fans is secure and vents outside.

Next, reflect on what you learned about venting the cavity behind the siding. The same process applies to your roof. During the heat of the day in summer, temperatures of a standard attic can soar making it possible for the air to hold huge amounts of water. If the nights are cold, this water must condense out as the air temperature drops. A cycle, if repeated often enough, will easily grow fungus and rot your timbers.

To avoid this process it is critical that an attic be well-ventilated and good ventilation relies on convection to drive it. Make sure that your soffits are clear and allow for the entry of fresh air. Often this passage gets blocked by extra layers of insulation or overzealous stuffing of insulation into these cavities. Finally, check the ridge, roof, or gable vents for any blockages from nesting birds or leaves.

Now it's time to go inside and look for moisture, again checking the obvious places first. Start by looking for leaks under sinks, behind toilets, and behind the washing machine. Take the kick plate off your dishwasher and look for damp areas under it. Check places that may accumulate condensation due to thermal bridging or breaks in the vapor barrier. These are often found around windows, doors, and cantilevered living spaces. Again these can be hard to spot sometimes since moisture can accumulate before it penetrates your living space but now that you are aware of the processes at work you should be able to detect the telltale signs early. If all these check out and you still have moisture problems, it's likely a ventilation issue which will be discussed in more detail in Chapter 5.

Before we take a final tour around the outside of your dwelling, let's touch again on why it's so important to become intimate with your house before you embark on your eco-renovation project.

Most people function on a limited budget and if these inspections reveal some serious problems, you might want to address them before you sink money into a facelift. It also spoils the fun if you discover these problems during an eco-renovation, as their remediation will likely add cost and cause delays. Finally, and this is what happened to us, your inspection might reveal that your house is past the point of no return and it's time to build new. In every case, proper inspections and maintenance procedures not only benefit the environment but can save you time, money, and safeguard your investment.

We have learned that the most common mistake in home design is to mismatch the longevity of materials on the exterior of the home. Chances are that is where you will find the most pressing maintenance tasks. In such a mismatch, the long-lived component will still look good in contrast to the worn out component right beside it. Home owners tend to postpone the replacement or repair of the short-lived component in the hopes that it will hang in there until the longer-lived component needs attention too. This is not only unsightly but can lead to bigger problems requiring more expensive solutions.

As you walk around your home, pay close attention to the western and eastern exposures. During the summer months when the sun is most ferocious they receive a direct hit. In contrast, the sun stands high in the sky midday, radiating its power on your southern exposure at a highly oblique angle. In the winter, when the sun does shine directly at your south-facing wall, it is not as intense. Consider any protection that trees or neighboring buildings provide and note the condition of flashing and other protective measures designed to shed water to the outside. Are they properly installed and capable of functioning as designed?

Although each house is unique, you have now familiarized yourself with your property and can produce or refine your own customized list of annual inspection and maintenance tasks. Remember, the main drivers of deterioration are solar radiation and moisture, nature's way of breaking down and recycling everything. By understanding and working with these natural processes you can extend the life of your home and reduce its overall footprint. Proper maintenance tasks may not seem green at first glance but they can take you a long way down the road to sustainability.

Exercise 5
Exterior: Inspection for Moisture Issues

Note: This list should become part of your annual home inspection. Identify potential problems before they become damaging and costly issues.

Yes	No	Check the Integrity of Building Materials and Systems
		Are perimeter drains functioning properly?
		Are rain leaders functioning properly?
		Are flashings intact and functioning properly?
		Is there a six- to eight-inch gap between the bottom of the siding and grade?
		Is roofing material intact?
		Are skylights functioning properly?
		Is the chimney and flashing functioning properly?

Additional notes:

Exercise 6
Interior: Inspection for Moisture Issues

Note: This list should become part of your annual home inspection. Identify potential problems before they become damaging and costly issues.

Basement and Crawl Space		
Yes	**No**	**Look for Moisture, Mold, and Old Water Stains**
		Is there moisture by the exterior walls where the floor joists rest on the sill plates?
		Are there water stains or mold around the sink, tub, and shower plumbing that comes through the ceiling?
		Are the edges of the carpet damp?
		Does the air smell of mold/mildew?
		Is the sump-pump functioning properly?
Main Level		
Yes	**No**	**Look for Moisture, Mold, and Old Water Stains**
		Check underneath the dishwasher (remove kick plate to look for damp areas under it).
		Check around washing machine (pull out to look for signs of moisture).
		Check under sinks.
		Check around tubs.
		Check around showers.
		Check behind toilets.
		Look for peeling or blistering wallpaper.
		Look for mold that reappears on walls.
		Look for mold around windows.
		Look for mold around doors.
		Look for mold in cantilevered living spaces.

Exercise 6 — Continued

Attic		
Yes	**No**	**Look for Moisture, Mold, and Old Water Stains**
		Check rafters, decking, and insulation.
		Are fans secure and do they vent outside (i.e., bathroom fans, stove fan)?
		Are soffits intact and clear of insulation?
		Check the ridge, roof, or gable vents for any blockages from nesting birds and leaves.

Additional notes:

5
Design Features to Improve the Livability of Your Home

"We feel 'at home' in our houses when where we live reflects who we are in our hearts."

— Sarah Susanka, Architect and Author,
The Not So Big House

In this chapter we explore more generally some of the ways you can improve the livability of your eco-home. By addressing these concepts we hope to build a sense of familiarity that will allow you to adapt them to your unique and personal eco-renovation.

1. Venting and Makeup Air

One of the well-known tests that are often performed to certify the sustainability of a home is the blower door test. It's a process where all the windows and doors are closed and a special fan is installed in a door frame that calibrates the flow of air with the resulting internal pressure drop to determine how much makeup air is drawn through the cracks and crevices of your house.

It assumes that houses are being built to a tighter and tighter standard to conserve energy and yet much of the current building code still mandates that people punch holes into their envelope. One of our pet peeves is the installation of makeup air vents consisting of nothing more than holes in the wall, usually close to the ceiling, that allow outside air to enter the home to replace that which is lost through dryer, bathroom, and kitchen fans.

Of course, providing this makeup air is especially important if the home contains a naturally aspirated combustion device such as a woodstove or gas fireplace. Without a dedicated vent, the makeup air in a tightly sealed home would be drawn down the chimney, resulting in deadly fumes entering the living spaces. From an ecological perspective this begs the question of why we would want to produce these deadly fumes in the first place, but let's just stick with the subject of ventilation for now, shall we?

The problem with many of these makeup air vents is that 24 hours a day, seven days a week, they allow warm air to escape the building whenever fans are not on. As we shall see shortly, convection is a powerful force and it does not rest. As warm air rises and accumulates under the ceiling it desperately wants to keep rising. A hole in the wall conveniently facilitates this upward mobility and the warmest air in the room is allowed to escape; hardly a recipe for energy conservation.

In our small-footprint home we decided to install an airlock for our makeup air. We don't have a woodstove or a gas fireplace but we did follow code and convention and installed bathroom and kitchen fans that vent to the outside (this was a decision we later regretted as we will discuss in more detail in Chapter 8). Our airlock consists of a 6-foot insulated box, mounted against the outside of the house in such a way as to cover the makeup air vent at its top. From there it extends downward to approximately floor level where a screen protects its opening at the bottom.

The concept behind the airlock is actually quite simple. Warm air rises. When fans are off and there is no pressure drop, warm air will escape out the vent until the top of the box is filled. Since warm air does not fall and cold air does not rise unless forced to do so, a state of equilibrium is soon established, preventing more warm air from escaping. Once a fan is activated in the house the resulting pressure drop easily overcomes this equilibrium, and the cool fresh makeup air flows into the house. As soon as the fan is switched off the equilibrium is reestablished and the airlock is secured once again.

2. Convection

The simple design of our airlock is a wonderful example of using natural forces to our full advantage. Before we explore some more examples in our "demonstration house," let's talk a little about convection.

At its most basic level convection occurs because warm air expands, and as it expands it becomes less dense or lighter. Conversely, cold air contracts and becomes more dense, or heavier.

When warm air rises (e.g., above a baseboard heater mounted on your wall) it creates a vacuum in the space it used to occupy. Cooler air rushes in to fill this vacuum, flowing across the floor towards the baseboard heater. This flow creates a vacuum where the cooler air had been. At the same time the warm air that has risen from the baseboard is deflected by the ceiling and starts to lose its warmth to the drywall. As it cools it becomes heavier and is inclined to start dropping. The vacuum below calls it to equalize the pressure and a full convection cycle is formed. (See Figure 1.)

This process drives air currents and weather patterns creating the trade winds and ocean currents. It has transported ships across the seven seas and has regulated the global climate for eons. Of course, it is never quite as simple as described; even walking across the room will disturb it somewhat, but it's a natural process that seeks to reestablish itself as soon as the disturbance passes. Recognizing this process and working with it rather than against it can pay huge dividends

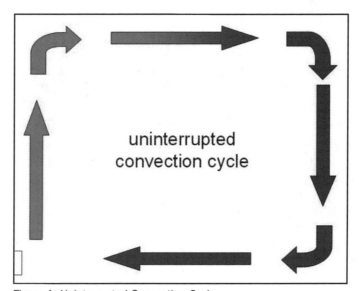

Figure 1: Uninterrupted Convection Cycle

in health, comfort, and energy savings. (See Exercise 7 at the end of this chapter.)

To illustrate this we want to share a couple of examples from our own design which you might be able to adapt to your eco-renovation project. Let us introduce you to Doug. Doug is a Christmas tree. Well, he started out as a Christmas tree. Now that he is 15 years old, he stands about 30 feet tall, directly in front of our north-facing inglenook windows. As you probably guessed, Doug is a Douglas fir and he is a living representative of the fine trees that were sustainably harvested and milled into the expanse of beams and roof decking that give our home its unique character.

Doug is also our air conditioner. Through another marvel of physics, the process of evaporation consumes energy or heat. Therefore the process of evapotranspiration — that is the evaporation and transpiration of moisture from the needles of our favorite fir tree — cools the surrounding air.

The interior of our home is open concept. The entire downstairs living area, except for the guest room which has its own little microclimate, is open to the upstairs through a broad stairwell. On a hot summer's day we simply open the inglenook windows to let the cool air from under Doug's canopy into the house while simultaneously opening some windows upstairs to let the warm air escape. A convection current is soon established which cools our entire downstairs to the comfort of a deep forest.

Since the top of the highest window we can open upstairs is only 7 feet, and the vaulted ceiling reaches to 13 feet at its peak, there is a pocket of warm air retained that we can utilize later in the day. On cool evenings, after closing the windows, we activate a circulating fan, pushing air through ducting embedded in the wall, to draw this warm air from its highest point under the upstairs ceiling and expel it across the floor of the inglenook downstairs.

On warm summer nights, air movement can be further enhanced by paying attention to wind direction and using casement windows to scoop air into the home, by opening them into the wind or using them to draw air out of the home by opening them downwind. In the winter we also allow warm air to naturally rise to the upstairs space and rather than fight the convection currents, we use our circulating fan to accelerate them. The faster the current flows the more homogeneous the air temperature becomes.

3. Visual Space

Our Douglas fir not only provides our air conditioning; it also adds ambience. As part of our forest landscape around the inglenook garden, Doug adds to the visual space of our cozy inglenook. Visual space is so important when designing your home and yet it is often neglected. When windows are covered with blinds or curtains, it limits our horizon and can make us feel cramped, and so we seek houses that are bloated to excess.

Visual space is all that space which lies beyond what you currently occupy. It can be in the same room, in an adjoining room, down a hallway, or outside. Put down your book for a moment, look around you, and then consider the following questions:

- What do you see?
- How much of the visual space you occupy is inside and how much is outside?
- How much of it is in the room you currently occupy and how much lies beyond? Take note where your eye is drawn naturally.
- What grabs your attention?
- How does it make you feel?

Since light travels in a straight line, the dimension of your visual space is determined by those items in your vicinity that block your view. If you are able to look beyond them, it can add a three-dimensional effect that enlarges your space, but if they dominate your attention, it can be distracting or unnerving. A good example of this is when you are sitting in a theater and the person in front of you is taller than you are. You find yourself moving from side to side because you can't see the stage due to the person's head blocking your sight line. An example of a positive effect of adding dimension to your space is a room with a spectacular ocean view framed in large windows. Your eye is drawn to the distant shore on the other side of the bay while you are comfortably nestled and secure inside your home.

We can utilize this effect to our advantage by carefully considering the everyday sight lines while designing our spaces. A sight line is that unobstructed line of sight between your eye and what you want or need to be looking at. Good, unobstructed sight lines are important in designing sport stadiums, lecture halls, movie theaters, traffic management and street layout.

Sight lines play a vital role in creating a visual space in your home and the effect that this space has on you. Remember that your eye sees everything even if you don't consciously register it in your mind. So managing your natural eye movement and what it is drawn to can have a profound impact of how a living space feels. You can even add a sense of mystery or exploration by intentionally creating sight lines that peek into unknown or off-limit spaces. If the sight line draws your eye to unpleasant or confusing imagery, it can be unnerving and may even make you feel uncomfortable. If a sight line draws your eye to a pleasing experience, even if just for a moment, it can elevate your mood. Moving a window, door, or wall just a few inches one way or the other can have a profound impact.

Light lines are a close cousin to sight lines. We use the term to describe the effect of shadows or sunbeams shifting across our space in rhythm with the earth's rotation. A small window, strategically placed, can throw a sunbeam on a vase and make it sparkle in the middle of winter. Another may mark the seasons by a thin ray of sun that dances across the textured walls. Light lines will happen whenever you put windows in a house, but all too often they are created by accident. Sometimes they are disruptive and so we block them, not realizing that sunshine is a natural mood enhancer, especially during the winter months. The mind covets these glimpses of visual laughter and remembers them as we make our way through the crowds or sit through boring meetings at work.

Once you tune into this concept you may want to design your visual space first and that may mean landscaping. We have a fetish for healthy food; we like eating it. For us it was imperative that the kitchen table and the kitchen sink, well, actually the entire kitchen, looks onto our urban farm (on a town lot) where many of the ingredients to our meals are grown. We visualized the fig trees in our courtyard, the grapes slung from the trellis over our outdoor dining terrace in our vineyard, and the old house turned into a garden cottage and workshop. All would be part of the vista that is framed in the large corner windows of our little five-by-seven-square-foot kitchen nook.

While the actual kitchen nook is small, the visual scope of this space makes it the largest dining room we have ever had. It also comes with some bonus features. During six months of the year the morning sun streams through the east-facing window just in time to illuminate our muesli for breakfast. During the other six months the winter sun streams across from the south as we eat our lunch. The space remains bright and airy with perfectly timed light infusion so that blinds and curtains are simply unnecessary.

Another example of extended living space through the maximization of sight lines can be experienced when ascending the three steps onto our front porch. Instead of a castle gate and drawbridge, you find yourself approaching a clear glass door and side light, flanked by a ship's bell that can be heard all the way to the "back forty"! We want our neighbors and friends to feel welcome in our home and so, as they reach for the bell rope, their gaze naturally travels across the 14-foot entry, through the patio window, and along the path that crosses the courtyard, until it arrives at the garden cottage.

If the cottage door happens to be open, their gaze continues through the workshop and into the greenhouse beyond. A wave and smile are reciprocated as we look up from our chop saw or potting table, or set our watering can under the fig trees, or lean the broom against the patio wall. No matter what the season or the activity, carefully planned sight lines can act like threads that connect us with our world and our friends.

Sight lines can also make a space seem larger or smaller than it actually is. Sometimes it's the grout lines in a tile floor that draw your eye across the room. Sometimes it's a striking photograph or a beam of sunlight that catches your attention in the distance. If these attractions are beyond our physical space, they literally expand our horizons. Conversely, if our views are restricted and everything we can see is in close proximity, our rooms may seem smaller than they actually are.

4. Strategic Illumination

At night you can also maximize your sight lines through strategic illumination. By illuminating primarily that which you want your eye to be drawn to you can actively manipulate your visual space and the mood it evokes. Lighting is a very powerful tool to help maximize any living space. If your eye is focused on close-up items, the space will seem cozy and intimate. If it's drawn to faraway corners of the room, it will feel grand and spacious. Lighting can be warm and inviting or cool and foreboding. When designing the lighting plan for your eco-renovation it's important to recognize that there are three primary functions of lighting:

- Safety lighting: The electrical code has rules about safety lighting, especially when it comes to illuminating your stairwell, and it is wise to follow or exceed these rules.
- Task lighting: This can include everything from a spotlight on artwork to desk lamps or even range hoods.
- Ambience lighting: As teenagers we used to call this "mood lighting," usually indirect or soft illumination that seeks to evoke emotion.

When we designed our lighting plan we worked from the old adage that you don't get a second chance to make a first impression. How often have you come home to a dark house with company in tow, later than anticipated, for a nightcap only to introduce them to your home in the glare of a lone hall light? Quickly you scamper about and turn on those lovely lamps you spent a fortune on, and rush back to snap that hall light off. No matter how agile you are, the moment is lost.

In considering all of our lighting needs we soon realized that we were able to integrate the three lighting functions by addressing ourselves primarily to task lighting. For example, on our inside landing you will find one dimmable switch within easy reach of the front door. Entering our home, a gentle touch activates four LED spots; one illuminates the "library" door (a bathroom door but designed not to look like one), one highlights an amazing, framed limited edition photograph called "Blood Red Star," one floods our bookshelves at the end of our multifunctional living space, and one spot highlights the hearth in our inglenook just around the corner. In an instant our guests are drawn to the focal points of the room as the entire space is bathed in a welcoming, soft glow.

We achieved the same effect upstairs where a single switch at the top of the stairs activates a rope light tucked into a ledge under the apex of our golden roof decking, a needle spot that sparkles off the vanity sink some 36 feet away, two wall lamps that frame our "Venus" window, (more on that later), and a spot that illuminates the balcony by reflecting its light off the three-foot overhang. Again the eye is drawn to all the highlights of this grand multifunction living space, as well as out onto the exterior area of the balcony.

Applying this kind of strategic lighting technique can result in fewer fixtures, reduced energy consumption, less wiring, and therefore less copper. If LED lights are chosen, the environmental benefits are multiplied. Each home is different of course, and an open-concept layout offers more opportunity to create extended sight lines with careful lighting design than a standard layout. If you remember that lighting is a powerful tool that can make your small home seem big, strategic lighting techniques can translate into real environmental benefits.

5. Placement of Windows

One measure to rate the quality of a living space is the number of walls that contain windows. By that measure, a room with windows on only one wall is rated lower than a room with windows on three of its walls. We found this measure most effective as we wanted to bring the outside in. It was one of the major contributing factors in our decision to forego traditional rooms and design our upstairs as an open-concept, multifunctional living space. Essentially, by allowing the sight lines to traverse three areas of activity (i.e., office, bed/workout room, and bathroom/laundry), each of these spaces feels much larger as it is free to draw on the light and ambience of the other two. With ten strategically placed windows over all four sides, it rates as a "class-four" space.

The sizing and placement of windows cannot be overstated as a key factor in designing your space. Western exposures will attract a lot of heat but mostly in summer when we generally don't want it unless it's a bathroom and you like taking showers in the evening. Eastern exposures will invite the morning sun which is great for early risers but less exciting for those intent on sleeping in. Southern exposures provide minimum heat gain in the summer because the sun is high in the sky but can flood your space with winter sun to elevate your mood. Northern exposures will drain a lot of energy from your home in winter with no chance of passive solar gain. Depending on your latitude, they can offer cooling breezes in the south and early morning or late evening sun in the north.

By sizing the windows properly you can choose to minimize or maximize these effects. Skylights can add yet another dimension but a word of caution: Traditional skylights have the potential of giving you a lot of solar gain when the sun stands high in summer, and because of their location and orientation to the night sky, can drain a lot of energy from your home in winter. If a skylight is desired, a sun tunnel skylight might be a better option. They are usually much simpler to retrofit and still offer natural light as an eco-alternative to illuminating dark rooms with electricity in the daytime. Installing both types of skylights can be treacherous. Great care must be taken so they don't leak. More sealant is not always better and thinking like a raindrop really helps.

Note that all these considerations have to be balanced with the primary reason we have windows in the first place; we want to look outside. It was while we were framing that we coined the name "Venus window" for our favorite portal. We wanted to be able to lie in bed and see the stars, an effect that promised to expand our bedroom on a cosmic scale. Our split shed roof mandated that the bottom of the main south-facing window be placed 5 feet from the floor. Since we had 13 feet to work with we were thrilled with the opportunity to create a 5-by-5 foot lens to the constellations. The first night after framing that wall section we looked through our rough opening and Venus happened to be perfectly centered in our field of view. The name stuck.

Now our Venus window not only enables us to gaze at the stars but it also provides us with weather forecasts when we wake to watch the puffy white clouds dance across the morning sky. However, this special window is not alone in its determination to expand our horizons. A smaller, vertically elongated version frames the majestic Poplar viewed from the bathroom and a south-facing transom window above the French doors leading to the balcony extends the view eastward to the California Redwood in the neighbor's yard.

Under both gable ends, and high enough to invite the rising and setting sun, two facsimiles of the transom window mark the time of day with changing light. Both are accompanied below by five-foot tall vertical casements that not only facilitate ventilation but offer a bird's eye view, or shall we say "cat's eye view," of neighborhood activities on our street; one sill has become the favorite napping spot for Cali, our aging feline.

Window trim in all its varied forms is another opportunity to manage the impact of windows. In many ways it can be similar to a frame around a painting. It captures the image of the great outdoors and displays it on the wall. In contrast, a bullnose and drywall-framed window draws the eye immediately outside without distraction or diversion. We chose the bullnose for all our upstairs windows. Opposite our Venus window we have two small north-facing windows immediately above our nightstands and sometimes when the cool night air wafts over us and the full moon bathes our world in a silvery glow it feels like we are sleeping outside.

One drawback to extra-large windows and transparent living spaces is that bees and birds sometimes fail to recognize the glass as the solid barrier that it is. We try to make it up to them by filling our gardens with natural habitat throughout the seasons. So it is not only the sky that offers a constantly changing panorama of life. The vegetable gardens and fruit trees on our urban farm offer not only visual enticements but auditory and olfactory sensations that remind us of our connectedness with nature. The early morning birdsongs and the sweet scent of blossoms always signal the start of spring.

6. The Home As a Sanctuary

In seeking escape from the humdrum of their daily lives, many people travel far and wide to vacation by the ocean, on mountains, in forests, or by the lake. People are drawn to nature and while nature has been commercialized in many ways, it is seldom that people escape to the shopping mall or big city to recharge their batteries. At some deeper level we recognize that we gain our strength from the natural world and seek its quiet confidence.

Your home has the potential to offer you that same confidence by becoming your sanctuary; a haven for your family. By manifesting your love in its care and designing it specifically to suit your family's needs and ideals, it can offer you a place of peace and tranquility where you can recharge from a hard day's work. A house can be so much more than just a shelter. It can be an expression of your values or a canvas bursting with your creativity. It can be a place of comfort and familiarity. It can even become a natural oasis in the noisy confusion of city life.

By making our home our sanctuary we have an indirect impact on lowering our carbon footprint by satisfying our need to recharge without the mental, financial, and ecological costs of airports and transcontinental flights. Focusing on sight lines as we design our eco-renovation or choose our next house, we recognize that our garden is as much an expression of our being as our home.

For us that meant full integration of our house design into our landscaping. We started with a plot plan that included not only the footprint of our home but the layout of our vegetable gardens, the location of our fruit trees, the native plants to fill the inglenook garden like the ferns and rhododendrons that complete our micro forest at Doug's feet, and the outbuildings and paths that lead to them. All were woven into of a grand design that we could hold in our hearts, working towards it as time and budget allows.

Unfortunately, when we stand at our kitchen sink, the large five-by-five-foot south-facing window in front of us still faces the wall of an old workshop. It is scheduled for deconstruction and the concrete pad that it rests on will indeed be refurbished into an outdoor terrace surrounded by those arbors dripping in grapes. Unfortunately that particular ideal will have to wait a little longer before we turn it into reality. Still, while life draws our attention to other priorities, we continue to hear the jovial toasts and laughter. They echo in our minds every time we reach for that light switch, prewired into our kitchen to activate the trellis lighting from inside.

How much water will it take to keep those grapes growing and keep that garden green? Since we have explored some sustainable design concepts that include extensive landscaping and a vibrant garden, in the next chapter let's examine some of the issues around water conservation and the selection of efficient and appropriate appliances for a greener home.

Exercise 7
Improving on the Livability of Your Home

This exercise will help you identify ways you can improve the livability of your home.

1. Take a good look around your home identify where natural convection takes place in your home:

   - Could you be making better use of natural convection in your home now?

   - Could you improve this when designing your eco-renovation?

   - If there is no natural convection in your home, how will you address this in your eco-renovation?

2. Visual space is all that space which lies beyond what you currently occupy. Measure five of the longest attractive sight lines in your home and take a look at the visual space in each room:

   - How could you improve this in your home right now?

   - How will you improve this in designing your eco-renovation?

3. Rate the quality of your living spaces by the number of walls that contain windows. List each room and document the number of windows and their placement:

   - Do you need to improve this in designing your eco-renovation?

   - Which windows will be replaced and with what type of window?

   - Where can windows be added?

6
Water Conservation and Appliances

"Every dollar you spend ... or don't *spend ... is a vote you cast for the world you want."*

— L.N. Smith, Author,
Sunrise Over Disney

Water is the most precious resource on our planet. Not because there isn't enough of it; after all there are an estimated 332 million cubic miles of water on the planet, but because 96 percent of it is found in the oceans. Of the 4 percent that remains, more than 1¾ percent is locked up in ice caps, glaciers, permafrost, and permanent snow and 1 percent is locked up in salty ground water. That leaves only 1¼ percent of all the earth's water (distributed between lakes, rivers, swamps, and the atmosphere) to supply our needs for drinking, irrigating farm crops, washing clothes, producing electricity, and flushing toilets. In this chapter we will explore how each of us can conserve this precious elixir of life. As you will see, selecting appropriate and efficient appliances is a big component of effective water conservation.

1. Water Conservation

In the United States, the per capita water consumption is about 100 gallons or 382 liters per day. In Canada it's slightly less at 343 liters per day but in countries like France it's less than half of that. Of that amount, more than 60 percent is consumed by clothes washers, toilets, and leaks, but the story gets even more complicated. In the US, only about 9 percent of the freshwater withdrawal is for residential use. Fully 37 percent is used for irrigation and 41 percent is used for cooling and steam production in the generation of thermoelectric power.

The mix also varies dramatically from region to region. For example, in the Okanagan basin of British Columbia, agriculture consumes 55 percent of the fresh water supply, and residential outdoor use for watering gardens and lawns and topping up swimming pools accounts for fully 24 percent of water usage. Residential indoor use in this region only represents about 7 percent of the total fresh water demand. It seems that our food, energy, and landscaping choices can have a much bigger impact on our total water consumption than low-flow toilets and efficient showerheads.

The trick is to take a holistic approach to water conservation. As with embodied energy our consumption habit drains our resources and that includes water. Yes, install low-flow toilets as part of your renovation; they can save up to 3 gallons or 12 liters per flush. Yes, install low-flow showerheads; they can reduce your water consumption in the shower by half. But of course there are other options, such as not flushing every single time you pee or taking showers less frequently.

The most important step in water conservation management is to become aware of where your water comes from. Is it from a rain-filled reservoir, a lake, a river, or a depleted aquifer? Depending on the time of year and the source of your fresh water you may simply be part of a diversion in the hydrological cycle that naturally circulates water from the ocean to the sky and back to the ocean. If you are draining a lake in an arid region or worse, an ancient aquifer, the situation can be much more critical.

2. Water Catchment Systems

One of the first things that comes to mind when talking about water conservation in an eco-renovation is capturing and storing rainwater. We already talked about the need to have an appropriate roof design that does not use toxic shingles or tar. Metal roofing is ideal. There are attachments for your downspout demonstrated at every home show and available at your local lumberyard that will divert the flow into a rain barrel. But before you decide that this solution is for you, let's look at the numbers.

Where we live we get a lot of rain. In the winter we can go for weeks without seeing the sun. So capturing rain seems like a no-brainer. We also have long periods of dryness. We can easily go for two months in the summer without more than a drizzle to cool us, so the first thing we did was look at our water bills and compare our summer and winter consumption rates. By subtracting our winter consumption from our summer usage we could get a good handle on how much water we used in summer for irrigation and, therefore, how much we needed to store for the dry period.

Your situation will be different but you can adapt this strategy to your circumstances. It turns out we use about 400 gallons of water per month in winter and about 1,250 gallons per month in summer. The difference, or about 850 gallons per month, is roughly what we use for irrigation. Since it's quite a bit more complex to capture rainwater for potable water than to simply use it to water your garden, we had hoped that we could capture enough water to at least take care of our vegetables.

According to World Weather Online, where we are, we get an average of about 12 millimeters of rain during the months of July and August. Our total roof area is about 1,200 square feet. If we capture every drop, this amounts to about 350 gallons per month. Since we consume about 850 gallons per month in July and August we would have to be able to store approximately 2,000 gallons to carry us comfortably through the summer.

Rain barrels range in size from 50 to 80 gallons. If we assume a 75-gallon capacity, we can calculate that we need about 26 rain barrels somewhere near the house to accumulate our garden's water supply. A better option would be to secure a 2,000-gallon water tank which requires a space about eight feet in diameter and seven feet high to accommodate it. Some may be able to house such a tank in an expanded garden shed, bury it underground, or embed it in the basement. Before you proceed you might want to check out the Green Housing section on the Canada Mortgage and Housing Corporation website, or the Harvest H^{2}O website in the US. Both offer information and detailed drawings for catchment systems.

For many of us, the good news is that we can have a tremendous impact on water conservation by adopting seemingly unrelated lifestyle habits. Eating lower on the food chain, by going vegetarian for example, reduces the demand for agricultural irrigation. According to the US Geological Survey (USGS) it takes between 4,000 and 18,000 gallons of water to produce the one-third pound of beef for your favorite hamburger.[1] Depending on where you live, going solar can save up to four times as much water as your total annual consumption by eliminating the need for thermal power generating plants.

3. Gray Water

Most of the water we use to shower, rinse dishes, or do laundry is more water than dirt when it leaves the house. Gray water is that component of our wastewater that is no longer fit for human consumption but also does not contain human waste. Water that does contain human waste (i.e., black water) contains pathogens that must be neutralized. This can be done by composting, heating, or processing in sewage treatment plants. Giving gray water a second chance to be productive is a great way to extend the hydrological cycle and reduce your total water demand.

Gray water can be used to flush toilets and water gardens but some jurisdictions prohibit its use indoors while others don't allow it at all. It's best to check with your local plumbing inspector during the planning stage. If you do live in one of the more progressive communities, there are a number of things you would want to consider to make the system work for you. Shower, sink, and laundry water may be easier to manage since it does not contain food solids from the kitchen sink. By minimizing organic matter it also makes it possible to store gray water for longer periods of time, if that is deemed necessary.

The most effective systems simply let the effluent seep continuously into your garden after transiting through a settling tank. Be careful if retrofitting your home with a gray-water system. Often low-flow toilets do not have enough water volume to transport feces along extended laterals without added flow from showers or sinks. Become familiar with your plumbing, do your research, or employ the skills of a local professional to avoid any problems down the road.

Combining a gray-water system with composting toilets not only eliminates this issue but it allows you to generate rich humus for your garden by turning the waste of one organism (you) into the food for another (your flowers). Composting toilets have come a long way in the last decade. Modern designs are stylish, odor-free, and low maintenance. They can fit perfectly into a renovation project where waste plumbing is difficult to retrofit. Again, check with your municipality before moving forward.

---

1 "How Much Water Does It Take to Grow a Hamburger?" US Geological Survey (USGS), accessed September 2014. http://water.usgs.gov/edu/sc1.html

4. Hot Water Tanks

There are two main challenges with hot water tanks. First, steel tanks break down over time and leak, needing to be replaced. Second, they lose heat if they are poorly insulated or the fiberglass insulation inside them gets wet. Both of these issues have been effectively addressed by modern tanks that are super insulated and offer a lifetime warranty. Any heat that does escape can help to heat your home in winter if you locate your hot water tank within your living space, as close as possible to the point of maximum hot water usage. Again, careful planning with your renovation can facilitate this.

If your tank has to be located a long distance from a fixture, it's better to run small-diameter pipe (half-inch instead of three-quarters) to minimize the amount of residual water in the pipe that will cool to ambient temperature between uses. To illustrate this point consider that three-quarter-inch PEX pipe, commonly used to supply water to your fixtures holds twice the volume per foot as a half-inch pipe. That means it will take twice as long to wait for the hot water to arrive at your tap.

Sizing your tank properly for your household is very important. It's not just about how much water you use but when you use it. If everyone showers at once, you need much more capacity than if you can schedule things across the run of the day. Choosing the temperature setting on your tank also has a huge effect on its capacity to meet your demand as you will see in a moment.

To help determine which tank size is right for you, it helps to understand how the water is heated. Although there are two elements in an electric tank only one of the two elements is ever on at a time. Under normal operating conditions, that would be the bottom element. As water is drawn from the top of the tank, new, cold water is brought in and it settles to the bottom. As the bottom element heats the cold water, it rises to the top where it can be drawn off. However, if all the hot water is drawn out of the tank, then it takes a long time to heat that large volume of water. That's when the tank switches to the top element. Now it can quickly heat just a bit of water at the top so you can wash your hands. After the top section is back up to temperature and ready for use, the tank automatically switches back to the bottom element to heat the rest of the tank.

The settings on these elements can be adjusted independently for desired results but you should be very careful. Some water tanks can be set to 175 degrees Fahrenheit (80 degrees Celsius), but since third-degree burns can happen to small children in only one or two seconds at 140 degrees Fahrenheit (60 degrees Celsius) this can be very dangerous indeed. It has been recommended that tanks be set to 120 degrees Fahrenheit (49 degrees Celsius) to reduce the danger of scalding but there is a catch. Legionnaires' disease, a form of pneumonia, is caused by Legionella bacteria which thrive in water that is maintained between 104 degrees Fahrenheit (40 degrees Celsius) and 122 degrees Fahrenheit (50 degrees Celsius).

Since the water temperature in your tank is never uniform it's almost impossible to balance these two risks unless one installs a temperature-mixing valve. When properly installed, usually just above your hot water tank, this valve takes very hot water from your tank and mixes it with cold water from your supply lines to generate a water flow that is warm enough for comfort but cool enough to avoid scalding. The only drawback to this solution is that dishwashers depend on very hot water to get your glasses sparkling and you may have to run a dedicated line, bypassing the temperature-mixing valve, from your tank to your dishwasher.

5. Tankless Water Heaters

Inline, on-demand, or tankless water heaters are often accepted as a de facto green option but they deserve a little more scrutiny. Here is why. The biggest challenge for electric utilities is to satisfy peak demand loads. Electricity does not store easily and the utility has to be ready for those peaks by securing enough generating capacity to meet them. One of the main objectives of a smart grid is to level out the peaks and valleys in the consumer load.

Most households use their hot water at approximately the same time. Early in the morning when everyone showers or in the evening when everyone is washing dishes and doing laundry. An inline water heater draws about 13,000 watts to produce four gallons per minute of hot water. In comparison, an electric hot water tank draws between 3,000 and 4,500 watts placing a much lower load on the electrical grid.

Gas-powered tankless systems place no load on the electrical grid at all but, as we already mentioned, burning gas does not solve the problem of CO^2 emissions. There is no confusion that burning gas produces less CO^2 than coal or oil but to say something is clean because it is less dirty doesn't stand up to much scrutiny. Again, it is important to explore the consequences up the supply chain to get a clear understanding of the environmental impact of our decisions. If you happen to live in one of those areas where coal is still used to generate electricity, you can still buy offsets for your electric hot water production and thereby support a solar or wind generating facility in a more progressive part of the country.

6. Appliances

Now let's see what we can do to make a difference when selecting appliances for our eco-renovation. Of course, you want to look at that big energy label on your appliances and compare their rated power consumption in the showroom. Equally important is to choose the right appliance for your needs. We'll go through them one at a time.

Consider your family's unique situation and design accordingly. Also check with your local utility for any incentives to upgrade your appliances before proceeding. Be mindful of the embodied energy and buy the best quality you can afford. Keep a close eye on the simple things. A fridge with a broken shelf in the door will find its way to the landfill long before the rest of it wears out. Make sure the unit is well designed and sturdy where it counts.

6.1 Clothes washers

Top-loading washers are just plain silly. They cannot achieve the velocities of front-loading machines so your clothes require much more drying time. They consume about twice as much water as a front-loading unit and their agitator can damage your clothes. Ever wonder where all that lint comes from in your dryer? It's produced in the agitation of your old-fashioned washing machine. Do yourself and the environment a favor and make the switch to a new, computerized front-loading machine.

6.2 Clothes dryers

We will talk about condensing dryers in the chapter on solar energy (see Chapter 8) because, believe it or not, your dryer is one of the key components if you want to go solar. The problem with dryers is that they produce unwanted heat in the summer and suck all the heat out of your home in the winter. If you have to have a regular dryer, put it in the garage or a workshop. Better yet, string up a clothesline in your backyard!

6.3 Refrigerators

There are many layouts to choose from, but perhaps the most important question when choosing a refrigerator is what size and how accessible the freezer should be. If you only use the freezer for groceries from your regular trips to the local supermarket, the freezer inside your fridge will serve you well. If you use a lot of ice or like to drink your water cold, an icemaker is important because it allows you to dispense both these items without opening the freezer. Beware though, the icemaker will take up a fair bit of space in the door and require filter cartridges that have to be replaced from time to time so make sure you actually need it.

6.4 Freezers

If you freeze large amounts of food during the harvest season, it pays to have an efficient top-loading chest freezer. Top loading is important because it does not allow the cold to fall out when you open the door and thereby conserves energy every time you access your stash.

Please don't put the freezer out into the garage. Many freezers will not cool properly if the ambient temperature is too low and the heat that they pump out of the icebox goes to heat your garage. If you build it into your pantry, you can retain that heat and apply it to the overall heating load of your home. Remember that if the power fails, your food spoils so it might be better to learn how to can your bounty. Spoiled or freezer burned food is never sustainable.

6.5 Dishwashers

The best use for a dishwasher in a modern home is to quickly hide all the dirty dishes when unexpected guests drop by. Unless you use toxic dish detergent, they don't really clean your dishes anyway, especially if food has had a chance to dry. So, you find yourself prerinsing or even prewashing everything before accumulating it in the dishwasher. That takes just about as much time and energy as washing them by hand.

Dishwashers are handy and ecologically superior only when you have a large gathering and you can fill them while the food is still moist and washes off easily. If that doesn't happen regularly, you might want to just pre-plumb for the dishwasher and fill the cavity under the counter with a roll-out island instead. That way you can change your mind if your needs change. Remember that once you have a dishwasher, you need to run it at least once a month to keep all the seals from drying out.

6.6 Counter appliances

Counter appliances are our favorite place to save on our carbon footprint in the kitchen. There is so much redundancy in small appliances and gadgets and they all use up space, resources, and energy to produce, store, and dispose of when they fail. And they do fail — a lot. When we look at the labor saving they offer, we seldom include the cleanup time or the fitness and dexterity training that comes with hands-on activities such as slicing onions finely, or kneading bread.

In the next chapter we will look at supply chains, product life cycles, and how to evaluate the ecological footprint of competing materials. We will continue to focus on examples to illustrate a process that you can apply to your unique circumstances.

7
Green Materials:
How to Evaluate the Claims
in a Changing World

"Our personal consumer choices have ecological, social, and spiritual consequences. It is time to re-examine some of our deeply held notions that underlie our lifestyles."

— David Suzuki, Environmentalist, Scientist

When you pick up any magazine and read about sustainable building and renovating techniques, the usual list of materials are mentioned, such as wool carpeting, recycled glass countertops, bamboo flooring, LED lighting, Forest Stewardship Council (FSC) certified products, etc. These are all important components to building or renovating sustainably and some have already gained such wide acceptance that they have become industry standards.

What is often missing is an in-depth look at the reason these items are more sustainable than others and a discussion of the complexity of that exploration. In writing this chapter, we were torn. Should we repeat that standard approach or should we step outside the box and offer an alternative way of evaluating the true sustainability of building materials? The fact is, this subject is a moving target and new technologies constantly offer alternatives to old approaches. The information, and therefore the list, that is relevant today will be outdated tomorrow.

We decided to take you into the weeds a little, but don't fret, we won't bore you with technical jargon and we won't overwhelm you with choices. In the topics discussed in this chapter, you may come across some new concepts that will pique your interest or spur you into delving deeper. You may also choose to skip over some ideas or products because you are familiar with them or because they don't apply to your situation. Just remember that any step you take towards more sustainable building materials is a good step. If you simply eliminate construction waste, you have already made a huge contribution to sustainable building.

1. The Progress Trap

We have already touched on the notion of embodied energy and how important it is to recognize the cost, not just financial but environmental, of your choices (see Chapter 1). In addition to the embodied energy, it is important to consider the environmental impact of the raw material extraction process. In this we draw on a concept that was planted in our minds by Ronald Wright, the author of *A Short History of Progress* (House of Anansi Press, 2004), among other fascinating works.

In Wright's 2004 Massey Lecture with the same title, he constantly refers to something he calls a "progress trap." A small village at the fork of a river is a good idea, but when that village grows into a city and paves over all the surrounding farmland while polluting the river, it becomes a bad idea. Humans are famous for turning innovation into progress traps, and Wright offers numerous examples in his work. Let's take a look why this is an important consideration when selecting building materials for your eco-renovation.

Our world has changed dramatically over the last two or three generations. When my grandfather was born in 1901 there were about 1.7 billion people on the planet. Now there are more than 7 billion, more than four times as many. Our old, tried-and-true ways are often like the proverbial village at the fork of a river. Now, collectively, we have grown into the epitome of the city that paves over perfectly good farmland. When assessing the environmental impacts of our choices we need to look beyond the obvious and that includes considering their impact if they get scaled up to world demand. The following topics are a few examples to illustrate this point.

2. Forest Stewardship Council® (FSC)

There was a time when regular lumber was a sustainable product. Then, as now, it sequestered carbon and our bucksaws were no threat to the huge expanse of forests around the globe. However, as demand grew for this versatile building material, and technology and scale exponentially increased, people began threatening the very survival of the forests with unsustainable monoculture and destructive logging practices. Now, with the growing recognition of the Forest Steward-ship Council®'s (FSC) certification program, we are trying to find a way to harvest our forests sustainably while still meeting global demand for the timber.

The Forest Stewardship Council is just one certification body among many but it is supported by organizations such as Greenpeace, National Wildlife Federation, World Wide Fund for Nature, and the Sierra Club. FSC certification is global in scope and is widely recognized for its diligent, comprehensive, and highly principled approach to forest stewardship. Nevertheless, even FSC has received some criticism for alleged unsustainable practices.

Is it better to buy FSC certified woods shipped half way round the world or better to purchase timbers that, while not FSC certified, are harvested locally by a small woodlot operator? In making these choices it helps to remember that there are no ultimate truths or simple answers. In the end, it's important to investigate where your lumber comes from and how it's harvested. Remember that no matter what your choice, each inquiry about the source of building materials and the environmental cost of its manufacture or harvesting, raises the awareness of sustainability in the supply chain.

3. Agriboard

Agriboard is a Structural Insulated Panel (SIP) that does not use Styrofoam. Instead it uses compressed agricultural fiber such as wheat or rice straw. It is considered very sustainable for a number of reasons: It uses a waste product that would otherwise rot in the fields, releasing its carbon content into the atmosphere or be burned which is also a negative carbon event. The manufacturer claims that agriboard has a negative carbon footprint as there is no waste in its manufacturing. The SIP does not contain formaldehyde and boasts increases in the overall tightness of the building envelope.

At the core of this concept is the straw bale which is currently a byproduct of grain farming. Since most grain is produced on an industrial scale, its production has a considerable carbon footprint. As long as the demand for straw is met by a byproduct or waste product of growing grain, it is a sustainable material but if the day should come when global demand for straw used in construction outperforms the supply of this byproduct and people start growing straw industrially as a building product, we will have created a progress trap.

4. Bamboo Flooring

Bamboo flooring is more ecologically beneficial to grow than hardwood. Moso bamboo is the most commonly used bamboo for flooring. It can grow up to four feet in 24 hours. It requires no irrigation in its native habitat and sequesters up to 70 percent more carbon each year than a hardwood forest.

Although the manufacturing of the actual flooring requires some industrial inputs, the environmental benefits of bamboo are often judged to outweigh this carbon cost. However there is a downside. As demand grows, more and more natural habitat will be sacrificed for bamboo plantations and local biodiversity will suffer.

5. Vinyl Windows

One decision that we found difficult to make when we built our home was choosing between wooden and vinyl windows. Wood seemed warmer and would match our Douglas fir roof decking and glulam beams, but vinyl offered the promise of low maintenance and durability.

We recognized the production process of vinyl has the potential to be quite toxic to the environment if it's not managed properly. However, the same could be said for certain wood finishes and there can be no doubt that wooden windows require frequent maintenance, especially if exposed to direct sunshine or placed on a tree-covered north-facing wall. One requires the prevention of drying and cracking while the other often calls for some intervention to prevent the growth of fungus. The compulsion to stray from sustainable practices to protect wood from these effects can be strong indeed.

Another challenge was the balancing of ecological benefit with our personal health. Most of us assume that if it's good for the environment, it's good for us, but that is not always the case. Our very existence tends to extract a price from the natural world around us. It can be a hard call but minimizing that toll and seeking ways to integrate 7 billion people into the natural life cycles of the planet is the aim of sustainable living.

We will explore the issue of windows and their energy efficiency in much detail in Chapter 8.

6. Drywall

Drywall, or gypsum board as it used to be known, was once made exclusively from gypsum mined in open-pit quarries such as the East Milford Quarry in Nova Scotia which lays claim to being the largest open-pit gypsum mine in the world. When acid rain was recognized as an environmental problem, scrubbers were installed in coal-powered generating stations to remove the sulfur from flue gas emissions. This process resulted in the production of synthetic gypsum as a by-product that has since replaced most natural gypsum in drywall panels.

The recycling of gypsum has become mainstream in many jurisdictions and plants like the one operated by New West Gypsum Recycling in British Columbia are rising to the challenge of closing the loop. According to its website, the amount of drywall waste that will be generated globally will rise from 11 million metric tons to 20 million by 2030. Its process captures this waste, separates the waste paper and metal for recycling, and returns the gypsum back into the supply stream to produce more drywall panels.[1]

Of course, there is still a carbon footprint associated with this process but since almost half of that total comes from construction waste and production scrap, we can do a lot to reduce it at the source. Ultimately the first step is still to reduce our consumption. Careful planning, great design, and building to last should always be our highest priorities; still it is encouraging to see how, by acting responsibly and thoughtfully, we can be part of, and support, a closed-loop supply chain that is striving to become more sustainable.

This also applies to many other interior products. While it is sustainable in the short term to use reclaimed or recycled products, we always need to keep an eye on scalability to be fully ecologically sound. When selecting any material always ask yourself, what if everybody selected this material? It may not dissuade you from your choice, but it sure helps put it into perspective. Ultimately we all need to climb on board and renovate sustainably. Supporting products that can handle this demand and remain eco-friendly is a good strategy.

---

1 "Recovery Process Waste Collection," New West Gypsum Recycling, accessed September 2014. http://www.nwgypsum.com/our-process

7. Siding

Since products used on the exterior of a house face much more demanding conditions and usually deteriorate much faster than interior products, let's take a closer look at one of the main consumers of material on the exterior of your home: siding. There are four primary choices for outside cladding in mainstream construction techniques:

- Wood.
- Vinyl.
- Stucco.
- Fiber cement.

There is some movement towards using steel in modern or commercial applications since it is very durable and can be readily recycled but most home owners are not yet comfortable with its appearance and prefer the more traditional feel of the above-mentioned options.

Wood is, of course, most durable when kept indoors. No matter how good your intentions, it requires a dedication to maintenance that is hard to ensure over time. If you use wood, remember to ensure that it was sustainably harvested preferably through an FSC-certified supply chain. When painting wood, you might want to consider the advice of a shipwright friend of ours: "There is only one white color." Painting wood a dark color will increase its heat absorption and contribute to the warping and cracking that is so common in sun-exposed wood surfaces.

Vinyl may be one of those choices where good for the environment may not be good for the humans involved. There is no confusion that vinyl will produce toxic pollutants including dioxin, a known human carcinogen, if it is incinerated or burned, perhaps in an accidental house fire. Often workers engaged in the manufacturing of PVC can be exposed to vinyl chloride, a clear gas that is another known carcinogen. There can also be no doubt that PVC is a durable product, light to transport, easy to recycle if kept clean, and requires little maintenance. Maybe it deserves to be a material of choice in some applications, such as windows, where the only alternative seems to be vertical grain or tropical woods, but not in siding where it can contribute significantly to the toxic flammability of your home or in flooring where many alternatives with lower VOC ratings are available.

Stucco, although an ancient technique for cladding structures, continues to evolve and its ecological profile remains in flux. Some are working on building a closed-loop supply chain while others have developed new versions of the stucco process. These are sometimes referred to as synthetic stucco but are really exterior insulation and finishing systems (EIFS). By the time you finish this book you will have the tools you need to sort through the merits of these materials including the obvious shortcoming of EIFS installations that place two vapor barriers on your exterior wall, trapping moisture between them, and all but guaranteeing rot and mold problems.

Fiber cement turned out to be our chosen compromise. We recognized that although the actual amount of cement in the boards is small, cement has a high carbon footprint at the manufacturing stage as it requires large amounts of electricity to power high-temperature kilns. We also realized that this electricity has the potential of being generated through sustainable means such as solar or wind in the future. Its longevity and low maintenance allow this carbon footprint to be spread over many decades, especially if it is installed with adequate care. We chose to predrill and hand-nail our boards in place to avoid prestressing the panels by using a nail gun. Our fear was that over time this common approach could cause the panels to split and release. Fiber cement board is also nontoxic and fully recyclable; although, there is some question as to whether it will ever mature to a closed-loop system.

One final option is stone. This may be the ultimate choice especially if it is indigenous to your area and you have the time, skill, and financial resources to become or employ a stonemason. It does assume a sense of permanence and as such relies once again on careful planning and design to ensure its application will be functional and beautiful for generations.

Each of these choices has different life expectancies, which may vary on all four exposures of your home. Be sure to give careful consideration to the implications of mixing these materials, especially in places that are hard to access. On the one hand, you may find that at ground level, under cover (i.e., inside your patio or porch), wood is the most sustainable option. On the other hand, you may find that stone is particularly suited for those dark locations where moss growth is inevitable and where stucco should be avoided. Fiber cement board might be perfect for those hard to reach gable ends if you remember not to trim it with spruce combing.

Don't be afraid to be eclectic. Use your imagination, combined with your own personal research. Pay attention to the microclimates of your lot and how they might change over the years. A tree could get taller and provide more shade or it could be cut down by a neighbor and expose your siding to full sun. Consider the changing weather patterns that climate change will bring. Take a walk around your neighborhood and see how other peoples' choices have weathered over the years. (See Exercise 8.)

There is an old adage that a chain is only as strong as its weakest link. Especially on exterior applications, it pays to find the right combination of materials that have well-matched life expectancies. Sustainability goes beyond color and style and demands an intimacy with the building materials of choice. Often maintenance tasks are triggered by the failure of a single part of an assembly or just one component of a system.

8. Quality and Cost

A good, functional, timeless design is still the most central issue to renovating sustainably. A close second would be the quality of the materials and the attention to detail and quality workmanship during installation. It's hard to wear out a marble counter, but if it is placed on top of shoddy cabinetry or cut to fit a poorly designed kitchen, its carbon footprint can be staggering.

Quality does not necessarily mean expensive; although, the old adage that there is "no free lunch" certainly holds true. The challenge is that there are quality products and then there are those made to look like quality products to the untrained eye. Often, corners are cut to save a few pennies in production, and that can render a product useless. We have an example of this in our upstairs bathroom. We wanted the look of oil-rubbed bronze for all the fixtures. We found a classic waterfall centerset bathroom sink faucet for the vanity and were thrilled that it matched the showerheads and mixing valve trim. However, a year after installation the paint — and it was paint — started to flake off the stainless drain plug. We are disappointed, but as we are committed enough to keeping things out of the landfill, we put up with this shortcoming. Most people wouldn't. A perfectly good faucet might be sacrificed because a matching drain assembly cannot be found.

No material is sustainable if it is only allowed to serve its purpose for a couple of years. Had we noticed the slight difference in the hue of the oil-rubbed bronze on the faucet and that of the drain plug, we might have spent a little more and bought a higher quality product.

9. Cradle-to-Cradle

When we evaluate the sustainability of our green materials it's good to reflect on an adapted and slightly modified version of the French artist, Paul Gauguin's famous questions:

Exercise 8
Green Materials: Exterior

This exercise will help you to familiarize yourself with your choices of materials and how they are used.

1. Take a good look around your home and identify three building materials in your home that can be easily recycled back into themselves.

2. Take a look at the four exposures of your home. For example, look at the life expectancies of cladding materials and choose ones you would employ for each of these four exposures of your home. Be sure to give careful consideration to the implications of mixing these materials.

3. Take a walk around your neighborhood to see how other peoples' cladding material choices have weathered over the years:

   • Why have some of them failed?

   • Why have some of them succeeded?

   • Are there any ideas or materials you will implement?

4. While walking around your neighborhood, look at other roofing material choices:

   • How many different roofing materials did you identify?

   • How many eco-friendly roofing materials did you identify?

5. Take a walk around your property:

   • What are the microclimates of your lot and how might they change over the years?

   • How will this affect your material choices?

   • How will this affect your urban agriculture planning?

- What is it?
- Where does it come from?
- Where is it going?

As we apply this to our building materials we will, one day, move from the notion of cradle-to-grave to the next step: cradle-to-cradle. This is the ultimate in building material sustainability, since it closes the loop, much like it's habitually done in nature.

A forest, a meadow, or a lake, left on its own, does not have a waste problem. It provides habitat, shelter, and sustenance for countless species in a closed loop of mutual benefit we call an ecosystem. One organism's waste becomes the food or shelter for another organism. The cycle is completed over and over again to the benefit of all. When we try to adapt our processes to this approach, we call it "biomimicry"; there have been some fantastic strides made in this field. However, biomimicry does not need to be confined to the laboratory or factory floor. We can become more aware of, and even employ the concept in, our everyday lives.

Selecting materials (e.g., metal roofing) that have the potential of forming part of a cradle-to-cradle supply loop contributes towards the development and ultimately widespread acceptance of this approach. Any material that can be easily reclaimed and reformed into essentially the same material again and again is clearly on the right path. Some materials, while not having that capacity, can act as feedstocks for other processes at the end of their useful lives. This is more complex and harder to trace but it can be an enlightening experience to try.

The more time you spend familiarizing yourself with the issues around each product, the better decisions you will make in the end. The exploration for, and discovery of, sustainable materials for your renovation can actually be a fun adventure. It was many a morning that we found ourselves, mug in hand and home-baked cookies at the ready, standing in line at the coffee machine of our local lumberyard, chatting with contractors. We have also been known to bring our lunch, set up camp in a big shopping cart, and spend the day at our local The Home Depot browsing the aisles and taking notes.

The Internet is a wealth of information and while it takes time to sift the useful from the superfluous, there is no substitute for research and being prepared. "Thinking like an astronaut," as Chris Hadfield likes to remind us, by working through all the possible consequences of your actions, is time well spent. At the very least, it will create a deeper connection with your home that simply cannot be matched by looking at a few paint chips at the hardware store.

As you make your decisions about sustainable building materials and practices always remember this important point: Contrary to how we might see ourselves, humans, by nature, do not seem to be rational creatures. Rather, we are rationalizing creatures. We tend to make our decisions on a limbic level and then seek data to rationalize our choices. Examples of this behavior abound all around us. It is easy for us to recognize it in others but much harder to see it in ourselves.

Even though it's hard, try to keep an open mind and explore all the possibilities before making your decision. Recognize your biases and draw on the vast array of information that is at your fingertips to gain a deeper understanding of the issues. Ask questions, lots of them, and listen to the answers. Explore the consequences, even the uncomfortable ones, and make sure that on a deeper level you are alright with them. Remember that you are voting with your wallet. (See Exercises 9 and 10 at the end of this chapter.)

Your decisions will add to the millions, perhaps billions of similar decisions made by others who are driving market demand for one solution over another. This is where change really happens. By adding your voice, and your hard-earned cash, to a sustainable supply chain, you are building a better future. Speaking of building a better future, in the next chapter we will explore a supply chain that can change the world and explain how you can be a part of it.

Exercise 9
Green Materials: Interior —
Use of Current Materials and Fixtures

This exercise will help you to identify what you have, and what you can reuse, repurpose, and recycle.

1. For your renovation project, identify the current materials in use (e.g., sheathing, insulation, drywall, metal, wood, doors, counters, trim):

   - What materials will you be using over again in your renovation?

   - What materials will you not be reusing? Will you sell, give away, recycle, or dispose of these materials?

   - Can you use these materials in other projects on your property?

2. For your renovation project, identify the current fixtures in use (e.g., lights, door handles, plumbing):

   - What fixtures will you be using over again in your renovation?

   - What fixtures will you not be reusing? Will you sell, give away, recycle, or dispose of these fixtures?

   - Can you use them in other projects on your property?

Exercise 10
Green Materials: Interior —
Components in Need of Replacing

This exercise can be used to identify what components you have; what you can reuse, repurpose, and recycle, and the reasons why.

1. Flooring:
   - What is the present flooring?
   - Why are you changing it?
   - What are you considering replacing it with and why?
   - What will you do with the old flooring?

2. Wall coverings:
   - What is the present wall covering?
   - Why are you changing it?
   - What are you considering utilizing instead and why?

3. Appliance:
   - What is the present appliance?
   - Why are you changing it?
   - What are you considering replacing it with and why?
   - What will you do with the old appliance?

4. Countertop:
   - What is the present countertop?
   - Why are you changing it?
   - What are you considering replacing it with and why?
   - What will you do with the old countertop?

5. Lighting fixture:
   - What is the present lighting fixture?
   - Why are you changing it?
   - What are you considering replacing it with and why?
   - What will you do with the old light fixture?

6. Plumbing fixtures:

   - What is the present plumbing fixture?

   - Why are you changing it?

   - What are you considering replacing it with and why?

   - What will you do with the old plumbing fixtures?

7. Furniture:

   - What is the present piece of furniture?

   - Why are you changing it?

   - What are you considering replacing it with and why?

   - What will you do with the old piece of furniture?

8
Getting Ready for the Solar Revolution and Why It Matters to You

"I'd put my money on the sun and solar energy. What a source of power! I hope we don't have to wait until oil and coal run out before we tackle that."

— Thomas Alva Edison, Inventor

The solar revolution, much like an industrial or a technological revolution, is not a protest movement but rather the next logical step in the evolution of humanity. Here is why: photosynthesis. Long before the industrial age, the economy of the planet was driven by solar power. Plants, as they grew, collected the energy from the sun and converted it into sugars to thrive. This was a very successful adaptation since the supply of solar energy is consistent and unimaginably abundant. Plants proliferated around the globe.

Because plants collected much more energy than they themselves needed in order to reproduce, plants soon shared their abundance with parasitic creatures that did not share the amazing capacity of photosynthesis. Plants could feed other organisms but they also emitted oxygen, a poisonous, flammable gas. The most successful parasites were those that could thrive by combining this gas with the sugars in plant matter to form energy that could drive their own metabolisms.

Animals, drawing on the bounty of plant life, proliferated as well. Soon they found that other animals further up the food chain saw them as easy prey and so this chain reaction continued to weave the web of life as we know it. As part of that web of life, quite high on the food chain but still totally dependent on the ability of plants to convert solar energy into calories, humans began their parasitic advance towards civilization.

Our global numbers languished at less than 10 million, about half the population of New York City today, until the dawn of agriculture. Then, even with the rise of ancient civilizations and their technological and social developments, it took another 10,000 years for the human population to reach 1 billion by the dawn of the industrial revolution. It was hard and treacherous work. The life of a parasite intent on squeezing every last bit of captured sunlight out of the ecosystem led to more than one social, ecological, and economic collapse along the way.

Eventually something extraordinary happened. In 1781, James Watt commercialized a steam engine that was capable of driving belts and gears to power industry. Fuelled by coal, which is nothing more than ancient sunlight stored deep in the earth for millions of years, this machine changed everything. Since we were now able to tap into this ancient bank account of solar energy, human populations started the staggering, exponential climb to the more than 7 billion that we are today.

As we all know, this reckless expansion has come at a cost. Although there are many consequences of this remittance across history, what has turned this into a classic progress trap is the imbalance that it creates in the fabric of life. Burning fossil fuels such as coal, oil, and natural gas disturbs the carbon cycle and thereby threatens the symbiotic dance of plant and animal (host and parasite) coexistence that we all enjoy.

Solar energy promises a remedy. Sure, it is still a small fraction of our total energy needs and we need to develop more clean energy storage options but according to research from Sandia National Laboratories, New Mexico, the amount of solar energy that strikes the earth in 90 minutes is as much as our entire world energy consumption was in 2001.[1] By capturing even a tiny fraction of this amount, through what

---

1 "Solar FAQs," Sandia National Laboratories; Jeff Tsao, Nate Lewis, and George Crabtree; accessed September 2014. http://www.sandia.gov/~jytsao/Solar FAQs.pdf

is essentially an abridged form of photosynthesis, solar power has the potential to drive our technological civilization without contributing to climate change or leaving a legacy of radioactive waste to future generations.

1. Early Innovators

Solar power has been part of our civilization for more than 2,000 years. The Roman Empire used solar ponds to harness the sun's energy to evaporate sea water and extract salt. Salt was such a precious commodity at that time that it was sometimes used as currency to pay Roman soldiers. The modern word "salary" still has its roots in this tradition.

Although solar power has been with us for a long time, early innovators and early adopters are still blazing the way as the potential of this technology takes hold in our modern economy. I remember being one of the early adopters in the computer world. I have clear recollections of paying thousands of dollars for a computer with 640k of RAM, two floppy drives, and a yellow screen that was barely legible. These computers were little more than trendy typewriters and there was no economic payback, ever.

Today's users of iPads and tablets mostly take these gadgets for granted but their affordability owes a huge debt to the willingness of early adopters to kick-start a now ubiquitous technology. In much the same way, future generations of users will depend on today's forward-thinking crowd to facilitate solar power that is affordable, reliable, and economically attractive. Thankfully we already have a couple of decades of this process behind us.

The microchip was invented in the 1950s, but it took 40 years until the widespread use of the graphical user interface launched the Internet as we know it today. In 1985 there were only 1,000 Internet hosts across the globe. In 1995 that number reached 1 million; today the number exceeds 1 billion. This stellar rise was facilitated by the fact that there were no competing technologies. There was no "dirty" Internet that had to be replaced. The computer revolution expanded into a vacuum.

Solar technology has not been so fortunate. Although the exploration of the photovoltaic effect dates back to the 1830s, it took until the 1960s for the technology to advance enough to find commercial applications, primarily in space flight. In 1985 the solar cell achieved 20 percent efficiency. Now, even with the competitive forces imposed by the fossil fuel industry, world production of photovoltaic components is doubling every two years. The technology also continues to improve. In a paper presented by Spectrolab Inc. at the 26th European Photovoltaic Solar Energy Conference in Hamburg, it was reported that photovoltaic cells had already achieved efficiencies of 40 percent.[2]

2. Passive Solar Energy

Clearly the solar revolution is underway, so let's find out how you can get on board. The first thing to recognize is that, as the Romans have shown, there are a number of ways to capture the energy of the sun. Everyone has utilized solar energy (e.g., drying a bathing suit while lying on a beach). This is generally referred to as "passive solar" and when it comes to home renovation, should be the first consideration.

2.1 Observe seasonal variations to maximize solar power

Passive solar is simply the act of maximizing the solar gain of your living space while minimizing its thermal loss. When it comes to space heating, maximizing passive solar capacity is the first step to renovating or building sustainably. It has to be done carefully since in most parts of North America cooling becomes an issue in the summer months, and the further north you live the more varied the sun's light becomes.

Where we are located, on southern Vancouver Island, just below the 49th parallel, the sun rises in the northeast and sets in the northwest during the height of summer. This exposes the north side of the house to some early morning and late evening sun while subjecting the east and west sides to the relentless heat and solar radiation of almost perpendicular rays. At solar high noon (which is not 12:00 because of daylight savings time), the sun stands just a few degrees to the south of the zenith in our sky. It is therefore possible to size our southern exposure overhangs so that just a narrow sliver of direct sun finds its way into our home at this time.

Conversely, in winter, when we need the sun and long for its rays to lift our spirits, sunlight streams almost horizontally through our south-facing windows while the north remains perpetually in shadow. The east and west receive only oblique radiation from sunsets and sunrises during the short days on either side of the solstice. Paying close attention to these seasonal variations where you live can prove vital for maximizing the solar efficiency of your home.

---

2 "Solar cell generations over 40% efficiency," 2012, R. R. King, D. Bhusari, D. Larrabee, X.Q. Liu, E. Rehder, K. Edmondson, H. Cotal, R. K. Jones, J. H. Ermer, C. M. Fetzer, D. C. Law and N. H. Karam; accessed September 2014. http://www.spectrolab.com/pv/support/Solar_Cell_Generations_over_40_Efficiency.pdf

While we were designing our eco-home, we built a scale model and set it out in the yard from time to time as the light changed to see how different times of the year and different times of the day would affect the amount of solar radiation penetrating our living space. If you have the time, you might want to do this too; it's fun and can engage the whole family. You can also do it as part of a thought experiment or have your architect simulate it for you. The important thing is that you find a way to really connect with the seasonality of light.

2.2 Windows and passive solar energy

Now let's look at the primary way that allows passive solar energy into your home. Single-pane windows are most effective at capturing solar energy. The problem is that they also allow energy to escape back outside during the night. It might be suggested that the most efficient way to capture solar energy is to have many single-pane, south-facing windows and cover them with tight fitting, insulated shutters when the sun does not shine. However, few of us would find such a configuration aesthetically pleasing or practical.

In our home, we have upgraded our windows to double-glazed panes, filled them with argon, and applied a low-e coating to the glass. Let's review these items one at a time. As we have already discussed, double-glazed windows have evolved from our experience with storm windows which improved our visibility and avoided the condensation and ice build up on the inside of the glass panes. Double-pane windows are simply an improved, modern, and more convenient version of this same approach.

The improvement lies largely in the fact that the space between the panes is now hermetically sealed which allows manufacturers to select the type of gas that is placed in this space. At minimum they fill the space with dehydrated air since the absence of water molecules reduces the air's conductivity and prevents condensation even on cold days. A further step is to replace this dehydrated air with an inert gas such as argon, xenon, or krypton. The overall effect is to reduce the conductivity of the window; that is, its ability to conduct heat through the space between the two panes of glass. However, double glazing has little effect on blocking radiant energy.

The final step in producing an energy-efficient window is to add the low-e coating. This coating is designed to minimize the amount of ultraviolet and infrared light that can penetrate the glass. Here it is helpful to remember that light from the sun is divided into three primary parts along its spectrum. Wavelengths from 310 to 380 nanometers (nm) comprise the Ultra Violet (UV) spectrum and are the ones that give you a sunburn and fade your furniture and carpets. Visible light ranges from 380 to 780 nm and heat energy or infrared light occupies the spectrum above 780 nm.

Solar radiation peters out above 2,000 nm whereas the objects in your home, like all terrestrial objects, radiate energy above this frequency. Since most objects in your home are at about 290 degrees Kelvin or 62 degrees Fahrenheit, they radiate at approximately 10,000 nm. Amazingly, glass is opaque to these frequencies and so there is no risk of radiating this energy out through the window at night.

Why then are windows so cold and how do low-e coatings help with heat loss in your passive solar home? Heat always moves to cold and there are three types of heat transfer:

- Radiation.
- Induction.
- Convection.

Although infrared heat at 10,000 nm cannot radiate through the glass, glass can conduct heat very well. So the heat that radiates against the inside surface of your inside pane of glass in your double-glazed window is quickly conducted through the glass and can radiate off the other side.

Since radiant heat energy can easily pass through a vacuum (the sun's rays do it all the time), it soon reaches the outside piece of glass which most helpfully conducts the heat to the outside. A low-e coating applied to the inside surface of the glass is designed to reduce this radiation and prevent heat from reaching the outside pane of glass. Simply put, low-e windows are designed to reduce radiant heat transmission between the two panes.

In a cold climate, this is beneficial when trying to reduce heat loss at night or during cold and cloudy periods without sacrificing the view. In hot climates this helps to minimize the heat penetration into the home and thereby reducing its cooling requirements. Adding a third pane of glass or triple glazing, can increase this effect even more. The addition of an extra cavity provides another argon-filled barrier to induction and an extra layer of low-e coatings to reduce radiation. In combination, these can double the insulating value of a window.

At first glance it would appear that if one is strictly trying to maximize solar gain, a low-e coating on the window could actually be detrimental. The higher the R-value the lower the solar gain after all. However, it all depends on how much sunshine you get in the winter. Direct solar radiation is much more powerful than simple heat loss of the ambient indoor temperature in your home. Even a few hours of direct sunlight can more than replace the heat lost through a double-glazed low-e window overnight. If there is no sun or the sun is blocked by surrounding buildings, there is no solar gain to offset the relentless heat loss and the low emissivity of low-e coatings becomes critical.

This difference is so pronounced that south-facing double-glazed windows with a low-e coating will provide a net seasonal energy gain in most parts of Canada, but only south-facing windows that receive direct sunlight. If not carefully placed, windows, much like fireplaces, can provide the illusion of heating your home while actually drawing heat out.

It's important to remember that there are actually two types of low-e coatings. One is specifically suited to hot climates while the other is suited to colder winters. Ask your window supplier about the Solar Heat Gain Coefficient (SHGC). The higher the number, the more heat you will gain. This can be a good thing or a bad thing depending on your predominant climate, the orientation of your windows, and the overhangs employed to keep out summer sun. You might even choose to mix and match your windows, choosing a low SHGC for west-facing windows and a high SGHC for south-facing windows.

When choosing the placement of windows it helps to remember that the R-value of your walls will always greatly exceed the R-value of your windows, even if they are triple glazed with a double layer of low-e coatings. Windows that allow you to gaze at your garden or expose that magnificent view can greatly improve your quality of life but there should be no confusion; only certain windows will achieve solar gain, the rest come at a cost.

2.3 Trombe wall

The Trombe wall deserves consideration in any eco-renovation that involves exterior work, especially if the exterior wall is facing south. It will no doubt be standard in home designs of the future. Quite simply it's a controlled airspace, much like the space created by the rainscreen under the siding that we discussed in Chapter 4, which is allowed to absorb heat during the day and release it at night.

The effect is intensified by placing glazing on the exterior wall of the cavity and creating a dark heat sink on the interior side. Two openings allow the warm air to enter the house at the top while cool air returns into the cavity at the bottom. Fans can be used to assist the natural convection-driven airflow and shutters are used to close the air passages at night to eliminate heat loss. An elegantly passive solution, this principle can also be retrofitted by purchasing preassembled panels made from recycled pop cans, or by making your own.

2.4 Heat Recovery Ventilation (HRV)

Now that we have captured as much heat as possible into our tightly controlled airspace it's time to address air quality. In Chapter 5, section 2., we discussed how to work with the natural forces of convection to keep the air moving in our home. We have also touched on the code requirements for bathroom and kitchen ventilation. Now let's take a closer look at the Heat Recovery Ventilation (HRV) system.

The objective of an HRV is to allow stagnant air in the home to be replaced with fresh air from outside without adversely affecting the desired indoor temperature. It can help a heated house retain its heat and a cooled house stay cool. Most HRVs accomplish this by forcing air through an alternating honeycomb pattern that allows the stale indoor air to exchange its heat energy with the fresh outdoor air as they transition through the unit. Condensation can often result. How the unit manages this condensation and the technologies it employs to minimize noise and allow for fine operating adjustments often determine the cost.

In many jurisdictions HRVs are mandated by the building code but even if they are not, they are an important part of an eco-renovation. Next time you visit your local home show, have a sales representative show you the inside of one and familiarize yourself with the many features available in the marketplace. You will live with your HRV for a long time and if it's not perfectly matched to your lifestyle, you will not be satisfied.

Usually HRVs function independently of your bathroom and kitchen fans. This can prove to be counterproductive though since some of the new, almost silent fans can move a lot of air. A bathroom fan extracting 90 cubic feet per minute (CFM) can theoretically empty a 12-by-14 foot room of all its air in 15 minutes. In reality there are restrictions in the piping that reduce airflow, and the location and availability of makeup air further affect the performance of the fan but it's a point that should not be overlooked. Exhaust fans will rob you of precious heat and ideally should be routed through an HRV as they are in most passive house designs.

2.5 Condensation dryers

Your clothes dryer is another, often overlooked, exhaust fan that moves a lot of air. If you are upgrading your laundry appliances as part of your eco-renovation, this is an ideal time to install an air-cooled condensation dryer. These units, long the norm in European households, don't require awkward hoses or external vents and can conserve energy by not expelling heated air from your home. They simply condense the moisture extracted from your laundry and collect it in a container that gets emptied after each load.

Although they might take a little longer to dry your clothes, air-cooled condensation dryers have the added benefit that the heat they generate contributes to meeting your overall heating load. Naturally this is not desirable on those hot and sticky summer days but as an ecologically aware home owner you may have already adopted the habit of hanging your laundry outside when the sun is shining.

The reason we need to consider things like clothes dryers in a chapter where we discuss going solar is that the first step has to be to maximize the retention of heat energy in your home. There is simply not enough roof area to heat a drafty, leaky, poorly insulated building with solar. Almost everything we do generates some amount of heat. Even while resting, our bodies produce about 100 watts of energy mostly in the form of heat; play with your dog and it's even more. If we can conserve as much of this energy as possible in the home without sacrificing air quality, solar heating can make a lot of sense.

2.6 Heat sinks

Before we get engaged in active forms of solar energy let's talk about heat sinks. These often come up in this context and are frequently touted as the panacea, or at least as a given necessity when going solar. To determine if that is true in your situation and your location let's explore how they work.

The basic principle behind a heat sink is that it stores heat when it is readily available and releases it at a later time when it is needed. It does this by transferring thermal energy from one mass to another. Joseph Fourier, a French mathematician and physicist who is often credited with discovering the greenhouse effect, pointed out that whenever there is a temperature gradient in a given mass of material, heat will be transferred from the higher temperature mass to the lower temperature mass in an effort to regain a state of equilibrium. We remember this with the sometimes counterintuitive phrase: Heat travels to cold.

The rate at which this occurs is determined by the thermal conductivity (TC) of the material. Aluminum and copper have a relatively high TC, rated at 205 and 401 respectively, whereas a common apple has a conductivity of only about 0.39. Of the two most common fluids readily available, water (0.58) is 20 times more conductive than air (0.024). The PEX pipe, which is commonly used to transport water in modern homes, is made from high-density polyethylene which has a conductivity between 0.42 and 0.51, roughly similar to that of water.

The rate of conductivity matters because it determines how quickly heat (sunshine) applied to the surface of a given mass (a slate tile floor) is conducted into that mass. Knowing that slate has a conductivity of 2.0 tells us that it could absorb the sun's energy rather quickly and transfer it to all parts of the tile in relatively short order. Proceeding with this example, since the slate tile is quite thin it cannot hold a very large amount of heat energy and so will cool quickly once the direct heat from the sun is removed.

Therefore, two important factors must be considered when choosing the material for the heat sink. First, you must identify its thermal conductivity; and second, you must consider its total mass. By understanding these two factors and considering the numbers above, the best thermal flooring might be made of slate tile laid on a four-inch think slab of copper. This would not only be cost prohibitive but ecologically irresponsible since copper mining puts quite a strain on the natural environment.

An alternative might be to use a concrete substrate, with a conductivity of 0.4 to 0.7, on which to lay slate tiles. This would slow the rate of absorption but it would also increase the time it takes for the heat to be radiated back into the room once the sun has set. You can adjust these rates by choosing your materials carefully, but whether fast or slow, this kind of passive heat sink works on its own clock. When the heat source is present, that is, when the sun hits it, it absorbs the heat but as soon as the sun is no longer supplying new heat, and the ambient temperature drops below the temperature of your heat sink, the stored heat is returned to the room.

An active heat sink allows you to delay this action and take some control of the cycle to suit your lifestyle. For example, you could embed some copper tubing in the concrete slab under the slate tile and connect that tubing to a super-insulated tank in a closed loop. Using a pump, you can move the water at your discretion between the slab and the tank. While the sun heats the slab, you are now able to move the heat energy to the tank. Then, many hours after the sun has set, or maybe even the next morning at breakfast, you are able to move warm water back from the tank to heat the slab and slate.

Active heat sinks are more costly than passive heat sinks but both require a great deal of planning if they are to work as expected. Much depends on your lifestyle, your local climate, the amount of direct solar energy you can capture in winter, and even whether you like to sleep with the windows open. If you like to sleep in a cool room, it might be best to move your bedroom downstairs and place the living room on the second story right next to that dormer you have by now converted to a sunroom. Such a layout would be a perfect scenario for either a passive or an active heat sink configuration.

2.7 In-floor heating systems

In-floor heating systems are often touted as inherently sustainable. This is not necessarily the case. Here again it's very important to look at the specifics of the design. If the in-floor system uses heat that comes from a cogeneration unit which generates electricity and heat by burning biogas produced from municipal composting facilities, it is definitely sustainable. Or if it's an electric system just for the bathroom to warm those tootsies when you step out of the shower with the electricity you generated from your solar array, that's good too. However, if it gets the heat from a gas-fired boiler, it still relies on ancient sunlight and exacerbates climate change by the expulsion of CO_2 into the atmosphere.

If in-floor heating is poorly designed it can waste a lot of energy too. Heat pipes embedded in concrete slabs will conduct heat in all directions including down and unless there is a barrier of insulation, the heat will radiate off the bottom of the slab as much as the top. In-floor heating systems, much like heat sinks, usually have considerable mass and therefore have a delayed heating reaction. Unlike a baseboard, for example, which can be turned off instantly, the heat in an in-floor system takes time to accumulate and to dissipate. Therefore, if your lifestyle or locale calls for open windows at night, even during the colder times of the year, in-floor heating may not be right for you.

2.8 Heat pumps

Heat pumps can be air-to-air or geothermal. Both function on the same principle that your refrigerator uses to draw the heat from inside the icebox and expel it into your kitchen. Since the process simply uses a compressor pump to move heat energy from one location to another, rather than creating the heat units itself, it achieves higher efficiencies than a furnace or boiler. However, these efficiencies are reliant on temperature differential and are reduced as the heat source becomes colder.

That is why geothermal is more effective than air-to-air, especially in cold climates. Six feet down in the ground seldom freezes and if there is water present, the heat transfer is accelerated. Unless you have a brook running through your property, geothermal can be cost prohibitive and logistically challenging. Air-to-air is much easier and less expensive to install but it can be noisy. Be sure to have your heat pump properly sized for your local climate and find a warm southern exposure for the outside unit to maximize your heat gain.

2.8 Micro wind

One final word about alternative energy sources before we discuss active solar systems in section **3.** Whether you choose to use them or not it pays to familiarize yourself with micro-wind technology. Micro-wind generators have been around for a long time and can produce considerable energy under the right conditions. Their major plus is that they produce energy at night and in winter when solar is, shall we say, challenged. Their main drawback is that unlike the large wind turbines on the hillsides, most micro designs still suffer from vibration and noise issues making them difficult to implement in an urban setting.

You may consider some vertical axis direct-drive models. They are quieter and produce less vibration but they are also less efficient. Always look for good mounting systems that can be incorporated in your house design. If you do have favorable wind conditions, the inverter issues discussed in section **3.2** also apply to wind power. Most turbines generate 12 or 24 volts DC that needs to be stepped up to house current. An alternative approach might be to identify or start a "community supported energy coalition" and invest in large wind turbines in your region.

3. Active Solar Energy

Now that we have explored numerous ways to reduce your home's energy requirement, let's take a look at the solar panels you have always dreamed would adorn your roof. Active solar systems generally come in two forms; solar thermal and photovoltaic (PV). Solar thermal captures the sun's rays directly to heat water or some other liquid, while PV panels use the photoelectric effect, first identified in 1839, to produce electricity. While both methods have been with us for a long time, they have been continually refined to achieve the efficiencies we see today.

Every time we convert energy from one form to another there is a certain loss in the conversion. For example, when you burn gasoline in your vehicle, only about 20 percent of the energy in the fuel is used to move your vehicle forward, and the other 80 percent is wasted in the form of heat. The efficiencies and economies of electric vehicles are based on flipping that equation so that 80 percent of the energy used actually propels the vehicle.

Experts in the field concur that too much emphasis is placed on the cost of solar panels, whether PV or thermal, and not enough attention is paid to the supporting control equipment, the efficiencies of the design, and the installation procedures. It pays to discuss these in detail with your installer well in advance to prevent any disappointments.

Some home owners also shy away from solar panels for fear that their mounts will cause the roof to leak, but qualified installers have tried and true mounting mechanisms. They will guarantee their work and carry liability insurance to protect you.

3.1 Solar thermal

Solar thermal has the capacity to directly capture a much larger percentage of the sun's energy than photovoltaic (PV) and while there is a lively debate in the marketplace about the impact of heat-pump water heaters on this discrepancy, properly designed and efficiently installed, solar thermal is still the most effective way of harnessing solar energy to heat water. To illustrate this consider that 43 square feet (4 square meters) of solar thermal collectors can harness about 2.6 kilowatts of energy (more than enough to heat your hot water for most of the year) and it takes about 265 square feet (24 square meters) to collect that same energy with commercially available PV panels.

Heating water for use in your home is the second biggest domestic demand load on your electric utility behind heating and cooling requirements. By taking care of this demand with a solar thermal system, you can maximize your roof space for photovoltaic capacity. Solar thermal hot-water systems can be seasonal or year round. They can heat potable water directly or use a drain-back or glycol system to transfer the heat to your water supply. They can also heat pool water and provide some space heating.

There are many variables that will affect your choice of solar thermal system. As a general rule, modular systems are better since they allow you to change individual components for maintenance or replacement whereas integrated systems can often be much more costly to repair. These systems incorporate various storage solutions and safety mechanisms; most come with a secondary storage tank to hold the preheated water before it enters your primary hot water tank. Pumps and controllers can also vary in design and longevity.

Thermal solar systems can easily be retrofitted to any hot water system already in place, so long as there is room. The supply lines (or line sets as they are often called) between the solar panels and the hot water storage tank are often run through closets or other hidden spaces on their way from the roof to the basement. Sometimes drywall has to be disturbed, so if you are doing some drywall work as part of your renovation, it's a great time to have your solar installer run these line sets. Solar Thermal lets you conserve that precious roof space so you can maximize your PV potential later.

3.2 Photovoltaic (PV)

Photovoltaic (PV) installations rely on inverters to convert the electricity and make it suitable for use in your home. Inverters require a separate breaker to tie into your fuse panel and that breaker has to be sized to match the capacity of your solar array. Inverters are often located near the panel for easy access and power cables have to be run from the solar array on the roof to your breaker panel. If you choose a grid-tie system a failsafe shutoff will be part of the solution, so that when the power goes down your system is automatically disconnected. That way your solar panels don't electrocute the repairman working on the lines outside.

PV can be susceptible to inconsistent sunshine since partial shade on a panel can greatly reduce its performance. Similarly, even partially shading one panel in an array can cause a performance drop. Here is why: Most string inverters in use will search for the optimal voltage/current for a string of panels. They will lock in to this voltage/current and ignore the rest. So if four out of ten panels lose even a little performance due to shading, 40 percent of the array's power can be lost.

At the time of this writing there are two solutions on the market to address this problem. One is known as a power optimizer which, while attached to each individual solar panel, works in conjunction with a single main inverter. The other is known as a micro-inverter which is attached to each panel and converts the DC voltage from the panel directly into AC right on the rooftop, eliminating the need for inline inverters. They make installation almost plug-and-play and it allows you to mix panels from different manufacturers, a real bonus if you have plans to add more panels later.

Another major boon to PV installations has been the widespread acceptance and implementation of "net metering." It used to be that harnessing solar power was limited by the ability to store electricity in our homes for use when we need it. This involved costly battery banks that often resulted in high maintenance costs. Net metering allows us to feed any surplus electricity back into the grid and bank it there for later use. The electricity we produce on our rooftop during those long summer days when we don't need it to heat our homes can be used by industry or other homes further south that might wish to use it to run their air conditioners.

Likewise, in winter when the sun is low and the skies are too cloudy to produce much solar power, we can draw on our banked kilowatts to run our heat pumps or baseboard heaters. Net metering allows us to transform our home from strictly being an energy user to being part of a smart grid where everyone feeds, and draws from, a common pool of energy. This form of distributed energy production takes its cue from the Internet.

4. Distributed Energy

The smarter utility companies have already realized that distributed energy is good for business. By downloading the cost of power generation to the home owner, they can focus on the profitable side of their business: The distribution of electricity. No more mega projects to finance, no more white elephants to amortize, no more environmental assessments or lawsuits, just a simple, clean business model where they get really good at storing and moving electricity.

The day is not far off when energy will be freely traded just like we trade information now. Before the Internet, back in the day of dumb terminals and mainframe computers, information emanated from a central point of origin. Even news came from just a couple of sources and was disseminated broadly among a passive audience. Like electricity today, information back then traveled in one direction only, from the producer to the consumer.

The free and open multidirectional information flow of the twenty-first century was not accomplished without some serious challenges and more than a little adaptation. Major players were forced to restructure or lose market share, consumers were encouraged to invest in hardware; the power shifted, and new success stories splashed across the headlines. With all this turmoil, few among us would advocate a return to the bad old days of centralized and controlled information.

Alternative energy solutions have advanced us to the point where we can start applying this same approach to energy production. By making your home more energy efficient, your eco-renovation project can move you a step closer to that goal. Maybe you can then envision yourself becoming an energy producer as well as a consumer.

In fact, net-zero building standards attempt to do just that. A net-zero home produces as much energy as it consumes over the run of a year; when it produces surplus energy it feeds it into the grid to offset its energy needs when the sun does not shine or the wind does not blow in its neighborhood. When the home produces more energy than it consumes over the year, it is called an energy-plus building. This requires an initial investment that may not offer immediate, stellar returns. However, we happily spend $9,000 per year on the luxury and convenience of owning a vehicle. We don't need to do this; we could live closer to work, take a bus, or ride a bike but we insist that a vehicle is necessary. We do it knowing that there is no payback, no value added, no return on investment, and it's bad for the environment. Spending just half that on greening your home will move you towards a net-zero house in short order.

Unlike another vehicle in the driveway, adding sustainable energy generation systems to your home will actually raise its value and make it increasingly more marketable. Insuring that your addition or new design incorporates solar friendly rooflines and other energy-saving solutions will prepare your home for the solar age. Whether you start with solar thermal to conserve roof space or decide to go 100 percent PV, your home can be part of the energy solution of the future.

Of course, your particular circumstances are unique. You may not be able to achieve net zero without resorting to purchasing some carbon offsets. One such company in Canada is Bullfrog Power (www.bullfrogpower.ca). They effectively channel your financial contribution to sustainable-energy projects across the country.

Bullfrog Power uses your contribution to match your power use with clean renewable power that is fed into the grid. If you think of the electricity grid as a big storage tank, you soon realize that by facilitating the contribution of green energy to that tank you have reduced the need to produce dirty energy to feed the grid. That's what carbon offsets are essentially about. In the US, you can easily check the fuel mix of your power utility by visiting the Environmental Protection Agency's website (www.epa.gov). As you can see there is much work to be done.

There are a growing number of such organizations across the US and Canada and many utilities even offer a green option to their clients. A small premium on your electricity bill is channeled directly to fund local sustainable energy generating capacity. Even if your home is nestled in the woods, you can be proud to know that all the energy you need to run it is produced locally through wind, solar, and micro-hydro installations.

You may need to implement your energy plan in stages over a period of time, as your budget allows, but be sure to make "solar ready" part of your renovation plans right from the beginning. If a subpanel or an expanded circuit panel is required to power your renovation, you should leave a couple of circuits open and at the ready to net meter your PV or wind-generating systems. If your water tank needs replacing or relocating, why not use the opportunity to prepare for a solar-thermal system?

Solar systems range in price and are evolving constantly, striving for greater efficiencies. Every eco-renovation project should explore the many opportunities to maximize solar gain. (See Exercise 11.) It's the right thing to do. If it costs a little more today than it will next year, consider that premium an investment in the future. In the next chapter we will explore the skills you already possess to invest in that future.

Exercise 11
Solar Revolution Checklist

Yes	No	Topics to Consider
		Do you have double-pane, low-e windows?
		When you are ready to replace your windows, can you repurpose the old windows in a greenhouse or another project?
		Do you know what type of new windows will replace the old windows? Consider the orientation of each window to determine what type of new window to use.
		Do you have a location on which to install a Trombe wall?
		Do you have a Heat Recovery Ventilator (HRV)?
		Are the home fans efficient?
		Do you need to replace your dryer? If so, consider a condensation dryer.
		Do you have an outside clothesline?
		Do you have an inside clothing-rack dryer for winter drying when the heat is on?
		Do you have a passive heat sink? Consider installing an active heat sink
		Have you researched micro-wind and heat-pump technologies for your locale?
		Do you need to replace your hot water tank? If so, consider replacing it with a super-insulated, lifetime warranty tank.

Exercise 11 — Continued

		Do you have a location for a secondary hot water tank for solar hot-water storage?
		Can you run line sets so you are ready for eventual solar installations?
		Is your roof solar ready? Is it pitched well and facing south or west? If a subpanel or an expanded circuit panel is required to power your renovation, leave a couple of circuits open and at the ready to net meter your photovoltaic or wind-generating systems.
		Have you considered a thermal solar system for your hot water needs?
		Have you considered a photovoltaic system for your electrical needs?
		Are you working toward net-zero achievement?
		Have you considered purchasing carbon-offsets?
		Is there a Community Energy Coalition in your area? If so, join the group. If not, have you considered starting a group for sharing ideas with other like-minded people?

Additional notes:

9
Do It Yourself or Hire a Contractor

"We gain strength, and courage, and confidence by each experience in which we really stop to look fear in the face … We must do that which we think we cannot."

— Eleanor Roosevelt,
Former First Lady of the United States

Everyone has a dream home: Maybe it's a place you saw on your last trip to Europe, your grandmother's house that you visited on your summer vacation when you were a kid, that welcoming bed and breakfast in San Francisco, or your best friend's summer home on the Cape. Maybe it's just a little cottage on the river you saw in a magazine. For each of us it's different but when we talk of a dream home, an image, a feeling, a sound, or maybe a smell pops instantly to mind.

Whatever it is, if we spend some time there, even just in our thoughts, we soon discover certain anomalies that are attractive to us. Take note of the light and the air as you enter a room. Are you drawn in or do you feel like an intruder? What is the first thing you touch? Where do you sit? Who is with you? Simple questions but if you ask them carefully, and answer them thoughtfully, you are starting to think like an architect.

By paying attention to the spaces that make us feel comfortable or recalling our favorite fort, hiding place, or hangout as a kid, we can learn a lot about the design concepts that speak to our inner self. Even taking note of the kind of restaurants we prefer, the stores we frequent, and the friends we like to visit most often, can tell us something about our architectural preferences.

How often do you hear that little voice in your head exclaiming: "What made them do that?" or "What were they thinking?" or "Wow, that's beautiful!" These may all be just off-hand judgmental remarks or they could be reactions to an inner-design concept that is just waiting to find expression.

When was the last time you went to a Home Show at your local arena? Did you sit around drinking coffee waiting for your spouse to find you again or did you work your way from booth to booth, looking for new ideas, exploring new concepts, and learning about new products in the market? What about The Home Depot, lumberyards, or hardware stores? Do you rush in and out buying only the essential items on your list or do you linger, browse the aisles, and maybe chat with staff or other customers to learn about things?

Most of us get a sense of satisfaction from doing things or at least thinking about doing things. The average drill gun in North America is used about 20 minutes in its life. We buy tools because we have a notion that we would like to use them. Lest you ladies think this is a "man" thing, take note of your studio, workshop, or kitchen and tell me that you regularly use every utensil, gadget, or tool you own!

The reason we often don't actually do stuff is because most of us have been trained that we can't. There is a wonderful program in California called The Tinkering School. It's like summer camp except that the kids get to "play" with real power tools and make stuff. Kids that begin by not knowing one end of a screwdriver from the other end up collaborating to build the most amazing projects. Why? Because someone has given them permission to try.

That is perhaps the first, and most important, step when embarking on an eco-renovation. You need to give yourself permission to try. No, you can't do it by yourself, no one can. Not the architect, builder, contractor, carpenter, or electrician. Everyone needs others to supply tools, materials, and know-how. Everyone has to take these components and combine them in the appropriate manner to get results. You are no different. You may be a sailor or an accountant, an administrative assistant or an inventory clerk, a rock climber or a truck driver. No matter your vocation or hobby you have skills that can be combined with the skills of others to make your project a success.

When we built "The Biggest Little House in Sidney," Laura took the lead. I had a little more experience but it was her property and her mortgage so she had to carry the consequences. I offered her the benefit of my experience and shared my perspective as we addressed each challenge but she made every single decision. From which fasteners to use, to the rooflines, and their orientation, it was up to her to call the shots. Still, it took a long time for her to realize that she was the one building the house. Even though she did not do everything herself, she was the spark that showed the way and the glue that held it all together.

1. Leverage Is Your Friend

You probably already know a whole lot more about building and renovating than you realize. Many of the skills needed are rooted in practical knowledge, reason, and diligence. Basic geometry and physics help to round things out but even these high school concepts are probably still slumbering somewhere deep in your mind. Let's take leverage as an example.

One of the challenges we faced when building was how to raise wall sections with just the two of us on the construction site. We are not burly folk and some would even consider us "old folks," but here we were, assembling two by sixes into framing sections that had to be stood up once they were complete. When we drew our plans we made sure none of the sections weighed more than 400 pounds but that was still way more than the two of us could lift.

We stood there for a while scratching our heads when we remembered a few words of wisdom from our building inspector. While we baked in the summer sun, struggling to remove forms from our concrete foundation, he chuckled and said: "Leverage is your friend." Just like when we were kids. Who does not remember sitting on a teeter-totter in a playground and how mom or dad or maybe an older sibling, would sit closer to the fulcrum to even out the weight? We laughed at the memories for a while and then went to work.

With a pry bar, which is just another leverage device used for pulling nails or prying things apart, we were able to lift one side of our wall section an inch off the ground. A little blocking and another lift, a little more blocking and another lift and soon we were able to get a couple of two by sixes positioned about two-thirds of the way along the two sides of the section. Now one-third of the wall's weight was balancing half of the other two-thirds of the wall's weight on our little teeter-totter.

Basic math confirmed that we now only had to lift 130 pounds to put a second set of blocks in place under the two sides, one-third of the way from the other end. With a little grunting and groaning we managed to accomplish this before realizing that all we had to do is have one of us sit on the short end to balance the load.

Now we were able to teeter-totter this 390-pound wall section higher and higher until we could easily tilt it vertical by removing one set of blocks. We did this without lifting a finger. Just like we did at the playground all those years ago, one of us would simply push down on one side and add as much body weight as required. Leverage really was our friend.

Thinking about, and applying, simple principles that you take for granted in your everyday life can empower you to do many things. The price you pay is time. The benefit is experience.

When we built our home we insisted on learning every trade and doing all the work ourselves. The process took five years but the experience has filled us with an inner calm that is fed by knowing that we can do stuff. We spent about 70 percent of our time studying, researching, and learning how to do something and only about 30 percent actually doing it but that knowledge base is something we will carry for the rest of our lives.

2. Safety Is Number One

There is another reason why time is the most important factor in a do-it-yourself project. It takes time to be safe, and safety should be at the forefront for anyone attempting any home renovation project. Exercising extreme caution at first can pay great dividends later. There is nothing worse than a close call or even worse, an accident, to frighten you off the construction site. Laura spent a whole day assembling her brand new chop saw, and she wore her bicycle helmet the first time she climbed into a rented bobcat.

A cautious start can build success and success can build confidence. That does not just apply to actually doing the framing. The same process can be applied to all tasks, large and small. Even hanging a bathroom mirror will go better if one actually takes the time to understand the job, thinks about what could go wrong, prepares for it ahead of time, and assembles all the appropriate tools necessary to get it done right.

At first it may only be small tasks, but this process has a way of building skills exponentially. The reason is that instead of just finding the most expeditious way of getting the job behind you, it focuses your mind on what is actually going on. We just looked at how leverage is your friend. That same knowledge base can help you hang a picture safely, if you take the time to really think about it.

Take a closer look at a standard picture hook you buy at the hardware store and you will notice that it's designed to direct the force of your Picasso as close as possible to the intersection between the nail and the drywall. Since the longer the lever, the greater the force, hanging a picture from the end of a nail places substantially greater forces on not only the nail but the drywall that is holding it secure.

Leverage, properly applied, is how relatively heavy pictures can be hung on small nails embedded in nothing but soft drywall. The picture hook directs the forces to the right spot and is constructed such that it actually angles the nail so that as more weight is applied the hook is pressed closer and closer to the drywall.

It's not just about building, the same process can help you gain the confidence to design your renovation, source your materials, draw up your building plans, and even choose your contractors, if you decide not to build it yourself. Understanding how things actually work helps you to accomplish all these tasks more easily. You don't have to do it alone. You don't even have to rely on friends or family members to show you how. We live in an age of information and in addition to the countless home improvement shows, renovation magazines, and books, there is the Internet.

The first time we laid laminate flooring we almost gave up. For a whole day we banged and cursed our way through one frustrating piece after another. We followed the directions and watched more than a dozen YouTube videos. They all told us the same thing. Snap it to the previous course and then give it a good whack with a special hammering jig to pop it in place. We tried and tried and all we were able to accomplish is to make a lot of scrap. We even decided that our laminate must be faulty because it just wouldn't go together the way it was supposed to.

After a long and frustrating day we searched some more and found a video with lilting Hawaiian music in the background. Not a word was spoken while two hands used three little sticks to lay laminate flooring effortlessly. We were awestruck and thankful that we could draw on a global community of people willing to share what they have learned. There are no surefire answers on the Internet but there is a lot of information and if you take the time to study it, much can be applied to your situation.

Building on the knowledge you already have can take another form. So often we think we need expensive tools, fancy gadgets, or complex software to get the job done. While it's true that some tasks go faster with special tools, when you include the time required to climb the learning curve on that new tool, it's often a wash. As it was with the laminate flooring puller, sometimes the fancy tools just drive you mad.

It's been 30 years since I learned how to use a spreadsheet. I've used it to build cash-flow projections for business plans, shopping lists, and everything in between. I'm at home in my spreadsheet and can't imagine life without it anymore. So naturally when we decided to draw up some plans, my spreadsheet happened to be on my computer screen. A couple of mouse clicks and I soon realized that my spreadsheet had drawing tools. Who would have thought that you could draw an entire set of blueprints, framing plans, electrical plans, and plumbing plans on a spreadsheet? Not me before that point. That is exactly what I did. The drawing tools allowed me to virtually mill my lumber and assemble it into wall sections right in front of my eyes. Stick by stick, lintel by lintel, we assembled the structure. Span tables in hand and the building code at the ready, we were able to think through every last detail.

It was tedious to be sure, but by the time I learned to operate the nail gun we had already built the house once. Let me tell you, it's much easier to move a stud or resize a room on the screen than it is to pull nails on the construction site. Much like preparing a business plan, the benefit was not so much in the finished product but in the process. Sure, the plans we presented to the building officials far exceeded their requirements but the real payback for all that time was the intimacy it created with our project.

The same holds true whether you do the work yourself or hire a professional to do it for you. The more involved you are in the process, the more proud you will be when it's finally done. There is a difference between creating something and just writing a check and buying it. Ask anyone who has knitted a sweater or built a rocking chair. When you do something with loving care, part of your being is embedded in your work. Whatever that is, it radiates back out into the world for a long time.

Here is one final point about doing the work yourself. As we have already mentioned, hanging out at The Home Depot or your lumberyard can be an education. Nothing beats touching and feeling the parts and materials you need to complete your project, and box stores like The Home Depot offer you that opportunity. But they don't have everything, and with the Internet, it's possible to research every last fixture, valve, wire, and switch on the market. Some of what you find will only be available through distribution.

If your project amounts to some serious money, you may want to formally ask for competing quotes from a few suppliers. It's a bit of work preparing a comprehensive materials list but it's also good discipline since it makes you think about every last detail of your project before you get started. There are multiple layers of pricing depending on volume and frequency of purchases. If your renovation is big enough, you can often get assigned a better price category by attaching a letter explaining the scope of your project. Don't worry about getting all the details right. Lumberyards and wholesalers know that they may not get the whole order all at once but if they are confident that they could become the supplier of choice, they will often sharpen their pencil.

The good news is that wholesalers who usually deal only with the trades will often do business with you, if you approach them right. Here are some tips:

- Respect that their primary customer is the tradesperson you are cutting out of the transaction, so wait your turn patiently at the parts counter and if you get bypassed for a guy who is slouched on the stool beside you, be OK with that.

- Recognize that you will not get as good a price as the tradesperson. There are many levels of pricing on the computer screen you can't see and a do-it-yourself (DIY) price is marginally higher than a trade price; however, it will usually still be a good price.

- Shop around. There are probably many wholesalers in your area servicing the trades. Some will be more accommodating (we won't say "friendly") than others.

- Don't expect them to explain things to you. They assume you know what you need and are simply buying it. Information costs money and they are not going to teach you how to install something so you can you cut out their main customer base. The best you can expect is an indicator like "this is the one we usually sell" or "that one is a special order." Now you know which one the trades normally use.

- Familiarity pays off. Once you have decided who treats you best, stick with that wholesaler for your whole project. Don't keep pinching pennies. You will get known at the counter and soon they will have a little more time for you. If you are friendly and lucky, you will even get to know one of the guys or gals behind the counter and they will grow interested in your project. Now they will move mountains for you.

3. Plan Your Renovation

"Whatever you do, don't build your house to code!" It was a mantra that Harry Pasternak repeated over and over and it still echoes in the chambers of my mind. "The code is there to protect you and prevent you from building something that will fall apart around your ears. Understand the code, respect the code, and then build beyond it if you want to create a home with lasting value." This is good advice to keep in mind even as you consider hiring a contractor or architect.

We have encouraged you to look beyond any self-imposed limitations and explore your latent potential, but before you snap on that tool belt let's take a look at the flip side of that coin. How can you avoid getting in over your head? The simple one word answer is: planning. We have already touched on this but it bears repeating here. Planning is not just saying: "We will renovate the kitchen next month." The benefit of planning is always in the process and never in the actual plan. Plans are truly meant to be changed as new information comes to light, new skills are acquired, or new materials are discovered.

The process of planning should not be rushed and, if at all possible, it should not be farmed out either. If an architect, designer, and/or contractor pats you on the head and assures you: "I will take care of everything," you should know you are already in trouble. Remember that you will live with the consequences long after that person has cashed your check. In order to communicate with professionals you have to understand their language.

If a plumber tells you that the stack vent is not sufficient to serve your addition and you need a vent stack, you should know what he or she is talking about before you balk at the additional expense. While it's good to ask questions, it's important you do some homework first. Unless you are prepared to pay for his or her time, you can't expect the plumber to teach you the trade.

4. Do Your Research before Hiring a Contractor

Good craftspeople, tradespeople, and/or seasoned professionals will take enough pride in their work to freely share their knowledge and approach. They will know what they know and know why they know it. However, they will have little patience for wasted time. If you really want to engage them, it may be best to pay them by the hour to consult with you before you let them get to work. Here is why: Most people who engage professionals simply are not that interested. They just want to get the job done. They have a rough idea of what they want and tend to rely on faith-based decision making to choose a contractor to make it happen.

What we're calling faith-based decision making is a common process where we get two or more opinions on something from two or more individuals and then decide which individual has the most credibility in our eyes. Once we choose the "trusted experts," we have faith in their knowledge of the subject and accept their advice, recommendation, or statement of fact without having any first-hand knowledge of the subject matter ourselves.

Most of the time this process serves us fairly well in our modern and increasingly complex world but it has obvious pitfalls. It is natural for us to be attracted to viewpoints we already hold and we may well find ourselves choosing experts that tell us what we want to hear. We may choose people who share our mannerisms or our way of speech because we feel comfortable in their company without paying much attention to their technical skills. We also may trust that these people have been practicing a trade for a long time so they must know what they are doing but that does not take into consideration that we are all different and some of us are content just repeating the same old mistakes, over and over again.

The most threatening experience for any professional is to be challenged by a layperson. For example, if a plumber or engineer is in a situation where it becomes clear that another member of the profession knows more than he or she does, it's no big deal. Professionals within a discipline learn from each other all the time. However, if that same professional finds that a layperson knows more about his or her specialty than he or she does, it can be very unnerving. This is especially true for an individual who relies too heavily on his or her professional certification and not enough on the knowledge or skill base that his or her accreditation is intended to certify.

This should not dissuade you from seeking individuals with appropriate credentials or checking them out with the Better Business Bureau, but it should alert you to the reality that the certification itself does not guarantee quality, knowledge, or skills and that just because they are not listed with the Bureau does not mean they are dishonest or incompetent. Some so-called certification programs are nothing more than a glorified registration or an affiliation to a professional group while others demand rigorous training and familiarization with established practices. It is difficult for any professional designation to certify the actual abilities of an individual holding that certification.

How do you identify those individuals who are truly dedicated to excellence? One way is to assume that if they cost more to hire, they must be better at what they do, but that still relies on a faith-based decision-making process. Another, and most commonly recommended, approach is to ask for references and talk to past clients of your prospective contractor. However, it is the rare professional who will put you in touch with a disgruntled customer. Even if you search online to see if there were any complaints filed against your chosen contractor, you will be hard pressed to determine if these complaints have any validity or are simply the result of unreasonable expectations or bad communication.

A third approach is to ask friends and family if they have someone they would recommend. But this can also be treacherous. Unless a job went terribly wrong few of us will admit, even to ourselves, that our choice in contractors was less than perfect. Besides, your needs are different from your neighbors; your personality, your budget, your attention to detail, your interest level, and even how much you will be involved on the jobsite, will all shape your relationship with your contractor.

There is a wonderful book by Carol Tavris and Elliot Aronson entitled: *Mistakes Were Made (But Not by Me)* (Harcourt, 2008) that is worth reading. It offers some striking examples of how cognitive biases can create positive feedback loops that lead to self deception. We all tend to make decisions based on our gut feelings and emotions and then justify them later with data carefully selected to support our decisions. It is helpful to be aware of this human tendency as it not only applies to you but also the tradesperson, builder, or architect you choose for your eco-renovation.

That is why investing the time to familiarize yourself with the materials, processes, and concepts that go into an eco-renovation can pay huge dividends when you select your contractor. Once you have drawn up your plans, explored and documented some of your design ideas, and made some decisions about the materials you would prefer, you are in a great position to engage in informed discussions with your tradespeople. This can greatly reduce the chances of miscommunication or misunderstandings and their inevitable associated costs. (See Exercise 12 at the end of this chapter.)

Don't expect them to be eager to engage. Every customer wants to talk but few have done their homework. Even fewer understand the challenges and issues faced by a discipline enough to discuss the merits of one approach over another. Professionals on the whole prefer to steer the conversation to what they assume to be its inevitable outcome. This saves time and money in the short term but it does not necessarily move us towards more sustainable building practices.

Eco-renovations are still a fairly new concept that many builders are just starting to tune into. Since they must guarantee their work, it would be bad business for them to recommend an approach or a technique that is unfamiliar to them. However, many builders we have talked to would like to build more sustainably, but find clients unwilling to share the risks of employing new technologies. They tend to stay with the old tried-and-true methods that may not be sustainable or eco-friendly.

4.1 Hire a contractor as a consultant

Once you have identified a contractor through the normal process focused on referrals and credentials, why not engage him or her as a consultant first. Ask the contractor what he or she would charge by the hour, to meet with you onsite, and discuss your plans in detail. It may take some convincing that you are sincere but skilled professionals will welcome the idea.

Any contractor realizes that some of their time has to be spent on meeting with prospects that may never turn into clients; it's part of doing business and a prerequisite for preparing an accurate quote, but the focus of that meeting tends to be on sales. Their purpose is not to explore ideas or discuss new opportunities to go green. Their purpose is to make a sale. Since that sale is not assured, the secondary purpose is expediency; sifting the serious clients from those just shopping around.

This represents an opportunity for you. By offering to pay for the contractor's time, a professional who is confident in his or her knowledge and abilities, can be enticed to discuss the merits and potential pitfalls of your renovation plans without constantly filtering the information exchange in favor of making a sale. A savvy contractor might offer to credit your consultancy payment, or at least part of it, towards the final contract price should he or she be successful in getting the work.

In any case, this approach creates an opportunity for a win-win situation. The contractor gets paid to share his or her expertise and explore new ideas in a risk-free environment. You get to discuss your concepts with a trained professional without concern that you are being sold down the river. Both of you have a chance to really get to know one another before any serious money is on the line.

4.2 Disputes with contractors

Most home owners don't realize how difficult it is to resolve a dispute with a tradesperson, a contractor, or an architect if they are not happy with the work. It's not like buying a product in which you can take it back for a refund. Once the contractor tears the drywall off your studs or cuts through an electrical cable, you are committed. As soon as the contractor puts on his or her tool belt, the person can invoke a builder's lien on a home owner's property if he or she doesn't get paid.

The primary remedy of withholding payment for shoddy workmanship or bad design is not an option, since a lien may require considerable legal expense to contest or remove. It's much more desirable for both parties to build a relationship based on trust. The last thing a professional needs is a disappointed or unhappy customer and the last thing you need is to change contractors halfway through your project.

An eco-renovation should be an enjoyable undertaking. After all, you are trying to do something positive, not only for yourself but for the community and the environment of which you are part. Creating a risk-free environment to openly discuss everything from construction waste to the detailed backstory of why one approach might be more costly or environmentally beneficial than another can prevent a lot of tension later.

This is also where your earlier efforts to get intimate with the trades, by at least exploring the possibility of doing the work yourself, can pay huge dividends. When we dug the hole for our foundation and moved the soil to the back of the lot, we learned firsthand that it was hard work to sit in that machine all day, with the vibration, noise, and diesel fumes. From pouring concrete to installing standing seam roofing panels we gained new respect for the skills and endurance that every tradesperson brings to the job.

The same thing goes for the careful selection of materials. Once you have gained a good understanding of the life cycle of construction materials and their environmental consequences, you can speak with confidence to their level of sustainability when discussing them with your architect or contractor.

No doubt the tradespeople will have a different perspective but you are no longer dependent on a leap of faith to evaluate whether their approach has merit. Not only does all that preparation give you the ability to know what questions to ask but it also helps you assess the scope of the project to make sure that you are not biting off more than you can chew. A pre-contract consultation may help you to plan long term and divide your eco-renovation into smaller phases that your budget can easily digest. Or, it may convince you to postpone the project for a period of time until a new technology is available.

There is nothing worse than running out of money in the middle of a project because of unexpected changes, cost overruns, or expensive delays. As is the case with all renovations, what promises to be an exciting adventure in sustainability can easily turn into a nightmare scenario filled with mounting regrets. The costs associated with a pre-contract consultation will reward you handsomely with peace of mind as you embark on your eco-renovation.

No, one person can't change the world, but now you know first-hand that one person can set an example, be an inspiration, and make a lasting contribution by simply doing things a little differently. By actively engaging yourself in seeking more sustainable solutions to age-old renovation challenges, you help to build a new standard and that feels good.

Exercise 12
Doing the Work Yourself or Hiring a Contractor

This exercise will help you determine if you should do it yourself or hire a contractor. Answer the following questions and make notes to review:

1. Have you ever drawn or seen a picture of your dream home? Make a list of the attributes of your dream home. How could you incorporate them into your present home?

2. What are the components of a renovation that interest you?

3. What are the components of a renovation that concern you?

4. What are the components of a renovation that frighten you into thinking that you won't be able to do it on your own?

5. What skills do you have that could be used in planning and doing your own eco-renovation?

Many people are not aware that their professional and hobby skills can be transferred into either planning or doing their own eco-renovation. Consider your skills and answer the following questions:

1. List skills from your profession that could be transferable to either planning or doing your eco-renovation.

2. List skills from your hobby that could be transferable to either planning or doing your eco-renovation.

Conclusion

Your eco-renovation has come in under budget and on time. Your home is transformed. Light has taken on a whole new meaning in your life and you mark the seasons by the changing hues that are drawn from your decor. Hot showers are more sensual because you know the water was heated by the sun. Long winter nights are cozier too, as you curl up with a good book, knowing the energy to heat your home is drawn from sustainable sources in exchange for your summertime contributions.

Your family is awestruck when they come to visit and highly appreciative as they nestle into that multipurpose guestroom. Your friends marvel at the ingenuity of your Trombe wall or the way your electricity flows back into the grid. Mold and condensation are a thing of the past and hot summer days are welcomed as refreshing breezes flow through your strategically placed windows.

The transformation is not only in your home. It reaches into the very core of your being. You know you have done a good thing. You know that you have contributed to the formation of a new paradigm. No longer do you see yourself as a bystander, disempowered by the complexities of modern life. No longer do you feel hopeless or discouraged by the environmental challenges faced by our global civilization.

So much of the human impact on our ecosystem stems from the design of our home. It's not just the materials that went into building it but also how comfortable we are inside its walls. A home that does not fulfill our needs leaves us searching for alternatives in our vacation travels, our socializing venues, and sometimes our transportation; all this searching leads to a higher carbon footprint.

Climate change is still a reality and CO^2 levels are rising. Arctic ice is still melting and storms are intensifying all over the globe. Ocean acidification continues to emerge as a primary threat to the global ecosystem by attacking the bottom of the food chain, and many are still oblivious to their contribution to this destruction of our cherished way of life.

You are not one of them. You have put your money where your heart is. You have acted responsibly to the best of your abilities. You find comfort in knowing that when your grandchildren ask what you did in the face of this mounting crisis you can tell them a story. It will be a story of trepidation, challenge, exploration, and triumph. Most importantly, it will be a story that lives on in the legacy of your home.

Download Kit

Please enter the URL you see in the box below into your computer web browser to access and download the kit.

> ‖ **www.self-counsel.com/updates/greenhome14kit.htm** ‖

The kit includes:

- Exercises to determine the livability of your community, home, and property
- Exercises to help you think about room use and renovation materials
- Solar Revolution Checklist
- — And more!